Quiltmaking for your home

Quiltmaking for your home

by Eileen Gonin and Jill Newton

Octopus Books

Thanks are due primarily to the American Museum in Britain, Bath, which has provided the source for many of the illustrations in this book. Its outstanding collection of American quilts has been our inspiration because we have been connected with it for several years and this has given us the incentive for further study. For what we have learned from reading we are grateful to Miss Avril Colby for her books **Quilting** and **Patchwork** (Batsford), to Mrs Ruth E. Finley for her **Old Patchwork Quilts and the Women Who Made Them** (Bell), to Marguerite Ickis for **The Standard Book of Quilt Making** (Dover Books) and to Fitzrandolph and Fletcher for **Quilting** (Dryad Press).

We are also indebted to Mrs Cathleen Maxwell, Mr and Mrs James Ayres and Mrs Micki MacCabe all of whom have allowed us to photograph their personal possessions, and to Mrs Irene Preston Miller, the Museum of Costume in Bath and the Welsh Folk Museum, St Fagans, Cardiff who have been kind enough to supply us with photographs.

Shiela Betterton and Eileen Gonin.

First published 1974 by
Octopus Books Limited
59 Grosvenor St, London W1

ISBN 0 7064 0349 5

Produced by Mandarin Publishers Limited
14 Westlands Road, Quarry Bay, Hong Kong
Printed in Hong Kong

Frontispiece: Hudson River Quilt, see page 11

Contents

Introduction

Not since Victorian times has needlework enjoyed the popularity that it has today. This remarkable revival of a craft that is one of the oldest in the world has, perhaps, something to do with the times in which we live and from which women, either separately in their own homes or in small and intimate groups, are seeking an escape – from mass production and from the surfeit of synthetic materials and standard designs that are such an integral part of contemporary life.

Of all the types of needlework that are staging a come-back the making of coverlets, so often misleadingly called 'quilts', is one of the most popular. 'Coverlet' from the French 'couvre lit', is a more accurate term than quilt because quilting is by no means an essential feature. The craze for making coverlets that has swept America has spread to this country and although quilting is still being practised it is primarily patchwork and its allied form of appliqué, or applied work, that are being so widely used. The common factor in these three techniques – quilting, patchwork and appliqué – is that they require only the simplest and most basic forms of stitch-craft, the ordinary running-stitch for quilting, over-sewing and hemming for patch and applied work. In this respect, therefore, they make far fewer demands than does embroidery in most of its forms, and the success of anything made by their use is far more in the field of imaginative design and planning than in strict technical skill.

Quilting is not only for bed-covers, it is ideal for small items, from cushions to cot-covers, whilst some beautiful hand-quilted evening skirts are also being made. Patchwork and appliqué go together, sometimes almost indistinguishable, and in this field there is no limit to the decorative possibilities. Each of these techniques will be described and explained in the following pages and although each can be used by itself it is usually in the combination of all three that the loveliest results are achieved. It is hoped by showing how easy quilting and patchwork really are that many, perhaps at present rather diffident needlewomen, will feel inspired to make a start.

Quilted Garments
A present day evening skirt in rich silk or an eighteenth century petticoat. Which?
It is, in fact, an authentic late 18th Century quilted petticoat from New England. It is regularly worn by Mrs Micki MacCabe of Westport, Connecticut when demonstrating the old crafts of spinning and weaving.
It is not a petticoat in the accepted sense but more of an underskirt, the dress worn over it being draped to the back so that most of the petticoat is revealed. Copied in any present day silky material, what an attractive evening skirt it would make!

(Courtesy of Mrs Micki MacCabe).

History of Quilt Making

The origins of quilting, the joining together of layers of fabric by running stitches, are lost in antiquity but are known to go back for 6,000 years at least. The word 'quilt' is derived from the Latin 'culcita' meaning a stuffed mattress or cushion and there are references to it by Varro, a writer of the first century B.C., but even 3,000 years before then it was a highly developed craft. This can be seen in a carved ivory figure of a Pharaoh of the First Dynasty, circa 3,400 B.C., who is shown wearing a quilted cloak. The earliest example of actual quilting so far discovered is a fragment of carpet found in a tomb in Siberia dating from the 1st Century B.C. Both these examples show a sophistication and artistry that suggest it was already an established craft. There is evidence of quilted jackets from ancient China–a far cry from the ubiquitous 'anorak' of today– and the craft spread through the Mohammedan world of Asia and thence to Europe.

In its earliest form quilting was utilitarian, for warmth and protection, and the stitches were purely functional for the purpose of securing a padding between two outer layers of fabric. As it developed over the centuries the stitches were gradually used to form patterns so that the decorative aspect came to predominate and frequently only two layers of material were held together by an elaborate all-over design. Inspiration for these patterns came from everyday objects–from flowers, leaves, shells, feathers–all combined in an ever-increasing intricacy to resemble wrought-iron or carving. Early in the story the patterns acquired regional characteristics so that those from the north of England differed from the Welsh–Northumberland, Durham and South Wales have always predominated as centres of quilting in Britain. Many of the traditionally regional patterns have survived to this day. Many crossed the Atlantic with the early settlers where they were often adapted and given other names, and where new ones of a more local character were added, so that there grew to be a wonderful richness in American quilting. In the very early days quilting was used to prevent chafing under armour–the Crusaders used it for this purpose. Later it became armour in its own right, heavily padded garments being used as protection against arrows. This being a domestic craft, a 'do-it-yourself' form of armour, it served as a cheap and practical alternative to the heavy and cumbersome chain-mail or plate armour of the Middle Ages, but even as late as 1607 the first colonists in Virginia found it effective against Indian attack. From providing protection quilting passed to being used for warmth, so that by the beginning of the 15th Century quilted garments of an everyday nature were being worn– cloaks and waistcoats for men, petticoats and caps for women. Examples of these can be seen on page 7. The earliest references to quilts in the form of bed-covers come from the end of the 13th Century but it was not until the 15th Century that quilted bed-covers were in common domestic use and were mentioned in wills and inventories. From that time onwards the craft was firmly established and in homes all over the country, both rich and poor, women turned their attention to the making of more and more elaborate quilts. The Quilting Frame was an essential item of equipment in many homes and from an early age girls learned how to use it, as they learned to spin and weave and bake, in fact to provide for all the necessities of domestic life. Because they were made to be used, very few of the early plain quilts still exist but fortunately the traditional patterns have survived.

As time went on the actual need for quilted bed-covers decreased, blankets became cheaper and easier to produce, so that from being a necessity of life quilts became something of a refinement. In some areas such as the north of England and Wales, however, the tradition of making plain quilts for ordinary family use has never died. In America even more than in this country the making of plain quilts gave way to patchwork which provided a greater outlet for artistic expression and for satisfying the need for colour and decoration in homes that lacked most of the trimmings enjoyed, not only by the rich in manor houses and stately homes, but by those who lived in cottages and farmhouses on this side of the Atlantic. As the popularity of patchwork increased so quilting on the whole declined, until it was often little more than a comparatively inconspicuous means of attaching the top to the lining. The inevitable exception to this rule, however, is to be seen in many American quilts where both the patchwork and the quilting achieved an equal standard of excellence—the lovely star design shown on page 47 is a typical example. Gone now are the days when many homes can boast a quilting frame. In present living conditions there is seldom the space for it and the quilting of a whole coverlet single handed, or even with help from daughters no longer given to sewing, is not a practical proposition. It has, therefore, become essentially a group or communal activity, something on the lines of the traditional American Quilting Bees. These gatherings were an important feature in the social life of 19th Century America. They were an occasion for the meeting together of women and girls who often lived solitary lives in the remote areas where the settlers were thinly spread. Patchwork 'tops', the completed outer layers, were stored away against the day when a daughter came to get married so that when these 'tops' were produced and the neighbours invited, it was tantamount to announcing a girl's engagement. The women would busy themselves round the quilting frame to convert the tops into quilts— sometimes with padding, sometimes with only a lining—every girl was supposed to have between ten and twelve with which to start her married life. Large families were an asset in those days! The last and final quilt was the marriage one which traditionally had a heart motif worked into it. While the women stitched and exchanged intimate gossip the children played and the men undoubtedly amused themselves, and the whole party extended well into the night with music and dancing. A contemporary example of a Marriage Quilt can be seen on page 11.

There has always been a strong tradition of quilting in the mining districts of the north of England and Wales where it was regarded as a much needed source of income. There were, in fact there still are, clubs which undertake work on a contract basis for customers. This communal quilting is still practised in America as well, where it is a popular method of raising money for charity, usually for churches. The now famous Hudson River Quilt shown on the frontispiece is a modern version of this idea which has also been revived in some more remote areas as a rural industry and some fine work is being produced in the mountain regions of Kentucky, Tennessee and Virginia. Quilting can now be done by sewing machine either privately or commercially – practical and efficient but lacking something of the charm and quality of hand stitching, but, governed by factors of time and space, it is a tendency that is on the increase. For practical purposes in the home, quilting is now usually confined to small items which can be worked on an embroidery or tapestry frame as illustrated on page 15, and this method is particularly suitable for cushions and cot covers.

In England traditional quilting techniques and the old patterns are being kept alive by groups of women in Women's Institutes and Townswomen's Guilds while in many parts of the country classes are held as a branch of Further Education. There is no need, however, for quilting only to look backwards because new and exciting patterns can be created and there is room even in this field for the purely abstract which, especially when combined with contemporary patchwork and appliqué, can be surprisingly effective – this again is shown in the Hudson River Quilt. For those who feel tempted to try their hand at the craft of quilting there should be inspiration in the fact that they are helping to maintain a tradition that has gone on without a break and without a change of technique for 6,000 years.

THE HUDSON RIVER QUILT
(illustrated on frontispiece)

Made between 1969 and 1972 this quilt is now famous in America. Thirty women embarked on the labour of love to help in the preservation of the Hudson River, all funds raised by its display going towards that good cause. Each block is the individual work of a different woman expressing what the river and its valley meant to her, only the clear blue of the river being used throughout to give an artistic unity to the whole. A few of the women were amateurs, most were professionals but all were inspired by a love of needle-work and deep concern for some project allied to river conservation. The quilt tells the story of the Hudson from its source in the Adirondack mountains in the top left hand corner right through to New York harbour at the bottom. Between are famous landmarks, Garrison Station, West Point, the George Washington Bridge

Marriage Quilt

A very short engagement meant that this quilt was made with remarkable speed. Although the bride-to-be was conscious of 'furtive sewing activity' on the part of her family and friends it was made as a surprise. Her mother, who was responsible for all the outer squares, devised the idea and undertook the final assembly. Each of the participants was given a 20 in square of white cotton rep and asked to produce an appliquéd motif of some particular significance for the bride. A clever if unorthodox short-cut was taken in asking each person to line her square completely as if it were a closed-up cushion cover – the lining is in brown and white checked gingham. These fully completed squares were then joined and the dark brown braid added to cover the joins. A delightful touch of fantasy is a secret pocket in which to keep 'money for the milkman' – to give away the secret, the hen's wing is a flap which opens like a small purse.

(Courtesy of Mr and Mrs James Ayres).

and Manhattan Skyline, while other squares show the plants, birds and fish or particular scenes that are significant to those who know and love the river. When all the squares were completed and joined together working sessions on the quilting were held at different homes along the length of the valley. A few of the women had never quilted before but each square was quilted by its maker giving a stamp of individuality to that aspect as well.

The inspiration for this fascinating project, and its co-ordinator, was Mrs Irene Preston Miller, a professional needlewoman herself, who is doing so much at her centre, 'The Niddy Noddy' at Croton-on-Hudson, to show her enthusiasm and to impart something of her skill to others.

How to Quilt

The methods described below are those traditionally used in quilting, and they are still often practised today. However for speed and convenience, quilting is often done nowadays on a sewing machine, which of course dispenses with the need for a frame.

TOOLS AND EQUIPMENT

1. Quilting Frame.
2. Chairs or trestles on which the frame can be rested.
3. Needles (No. 9 betweens).
4. Tacking cotton and No. 40 cotton.
5. Large yarn needle.
6. Piece of tailor's chalk.
7. Several yards of tape.
8. A 'top' either plain material or combination of patchwork, appliqué and plain material.
9. Backing material.
10. Filling or wadding.

MATERIALS

Top

For the traditional wadded quilt, where the sewn design is completely reversible, the top and backing should be of the same quality material. It should be smooth and soft, preferably with a sheen, but not shiny. Sateen, poplin, dull satin and silk are all good. If however, the top is pieced and/or appliquéd, then an inferior material, such as calico, can be used for the backing, as, in this case, the quilt will not be reversible.

Do not have a seam down the centre of the top. If two widths are needed, split one width down the middle and sew a half to each side of the centre panel.

Filling

The filling can be of well washed, carded sheep's wool, cotton wool or the modern polyester waddings.

FRAME

The quilting frame consists of two long bars of wood called rails and two short pieces which are stretchers. The stretchers fit into slots in the rails and are held in place by wooden pegs fixed in holes. Occasionally the quilting frame rests on its own trestles, more usually it rests on the tops of two straight-backed chairs. For a full sized quilt the frame should be at least 90 ins long. A frame 36 ins long is sufficient for making cot quilts and cushion covers.

A piece of webbing or braid is tacked to the inner edge of each of the rails. For small pieces of work a large embroidery frame can be used, provided it rests on a stand, as it is essential to have both hands free for the work.

METHOD OF WORKING

If making a big quilt all seams must be sewn and pressed flat before quilting. All appliqué and patchwork must be finished and the patterned 'top' treated as one piece of material.

For a smaller item, i.e. a tea cosy, the outline of the finished article should be marked on the top material before starting to work. It should not be cut out until the quilting has been completed as sometimes the work can twist slightly out of shape.

PATTERNS

In deciding which patterns to use, thought must be given to the uses to

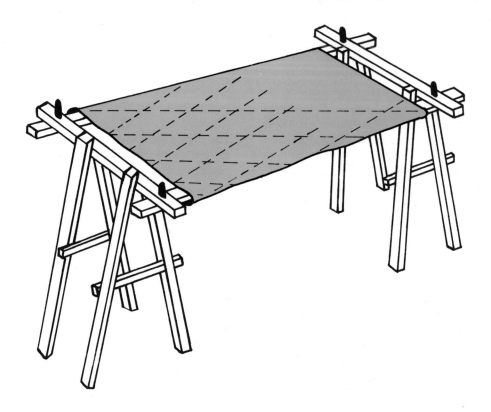

Traditional Quilting Frame

which the finished article will be put. A cushion cover should have the principal emphasis in the centre, while on a bed quilt the centre pattern should fit the top of the bed.

Although in days gone by an experienced quilter would seldom make sketches of the general plan, it would be helpful to do so. It must be remembered that the sewing, in addition to being decorative, is used to hold the three layers together, so that the maximum unquilted spaces should be approximately two inches across. Templates should be firm, and can be made of cardboard, metal or plastic. Patterns can be built up from simple shapes, or traditional ones used. It is advisable to draw the chosen design on paper before transferring it to the cardboard or metal from which the template is to be cut.

MARKING

Having decided upon the patterns to be used, they are marked out on the top before setting it in the frame. Spread the top over a thick blanket on a table or on the floor. Be sure to mark the centre line and any other relevant points. Place the appropriate template in position and mark round it with the yarn needle which is held almost flat on the material so that it makes a slight crease in the surface. Any awkward

Frames

Ideal for quilting small articles the tapestry frame is shown here with a typical Pennsylvania German motif in appliqué which is in the process of being quilted. The small embroidery frame has been used for applying the star – many people prefer to do appliqué with a frame.

(Courtesy of Mrs Micki MacCabe).

patterns can be marked in tailor's chalk which is easily removed. On no account use pencil, as pencil marks are very difficult to wash out. When using a pattern with straight lines these should be parallel. When interrupted by another pattern they should continue on the other side just as if there had been no break.

As·a rule the solid lines shown on the template are marked in, and the dotted lines sewn in freehand.

SETTING UP

When the pattern has been marked the work is set in the frame.

1. With the frame still in four separate pieces the backing material should be sewn at both ends to the webbing which is attached to the rails. The material should then be rolled round

must be laid on piece by piece to give an even thickness. Only enough wool to cover the 18 in width can be laid on at any one time, and each time the quilt is rolled on, more wool must be added.

3. The top, with the pattern already marked is then laid on to fit exactly, and firmly tacked along the side next to the front rail, the tacking going through all three layers. It should be fastened along the far side with plenty of pins, or needles used as pins. The weight of the filling and top hanging over the far rail helps to keep the material taut.

4. One end of the tape is tied round a stretcher, close to the rail, taken across and pinned on to the edge of the work, through the three layers, looped round the stretcher again,

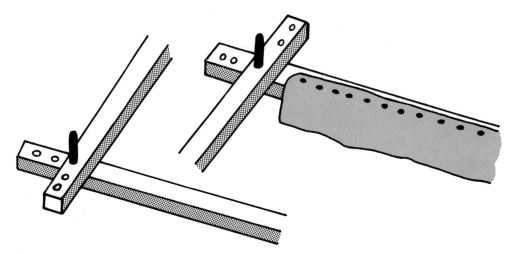

one rail until only 18 ins is left exposed. The stretchers are then fixed in through the slots in the rails and the four pegs inserted. The work should not be too tight.

2. The padding is next laid on. Cotton wool or wadding should be warmed to make it fluffy and laid on carefully and evenly. The sheets of wadding are not cut, but allowed to hang over the far rail. Carded wool

then pinned to the work a few inches farther on. Continue in this way to the end. Treat the other edge in the same way so that the work is firmly held.

5. Sewing should be done with a No. 40 or finer cotton (not mercerised cotton) or pure silk, to match the top, with a No. 8 or No. 9 (betweens) needle.

6. The quilting frame should be at a

Top Material is tacked in place next to the front rail

height convenient to the worker. The sewing is done in small, even running stitches which must go through all three layers of material. Regularity of stitch size is the most important thing in quilting. The most accurate way to work is to keep one hand beneath the work, and push the needle vertically down through the layers of material from the top. The needle is then pushed back up through the work from the underneath to complete the stitch. It is a slow laborious business, and with more experience, several stitches can be taken before the needle is pulled away from the work. Knots at the beginning and end of the thread should be drawn through to the wadding so they do not show on either side.

7. When the portion of the quilt in the frame has been sewn, the quilt must be 'rolled'. The tapes and pins at the far side of the work are taken out. The sewn part is then carefully rolled round the near rail exposing another length of the unsewn portion of the quilt. This is then fixed in the same way as before. Continue in this way until the whole quilt has been sewn.

FINISHING

There are three methods of finishing the edges.

1. When the quilt is taken out of the frame, the edges of the top and backing are turned in and a line of running stitch worked as near to the edge as possible. Make sure the padding does go right to the edge. Run a second row of stitching one quarter of an inch inside the first.

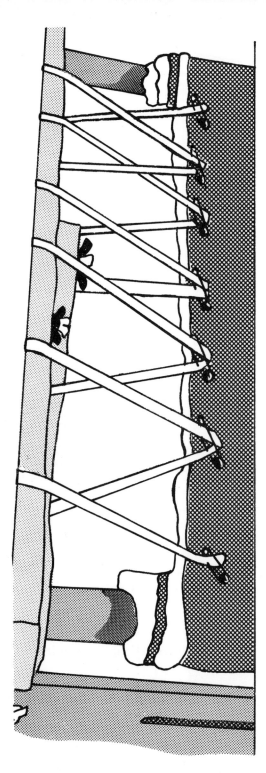

Sides of the work are kept taut by tapes pinned round the rail

2. For cushion covers and tea cosies and sometimes cot quilts, a piped edge is used. The piping cord (pre-shrunk) is covered and sewn on in the usual way.
3. On many American quilts the edge is bound. The backing material has been cut slightly larger than the top. It is then turned over the top and hemmed down.
   Alternatively the edges are trimmed and bound with a bias strip cut in the same or matching material as the top.

TRAPUNTO OR STUFFED QUILTING

These are, in fact, the same but the term Stuffed Quilting is more usual these days.

Materials

Any good closely woven material can be used for the top but the backing must be of muslin or scrim or anything in a coarse weave that is not too thick. For the stuffing a small quantity of soft wool or cottonwool is required.

Method

The pattern is marked out as in ordinary quilting and then worked in the usual way but some people prefer to use small back stitches rather than running stitches for this type of quilting. When the outline is worked and it is decided which areas of the design are to be stuffed the muslin (or backing) is parted and small pieces of

Quilted Garments
The two silk petticoats shown opposite are elaborately quilted and are in marked contrast to the much simpler example from New England illustrated on page 7 – evidence of a more sophisticated style of life in England. They date from around 1750, the cream one showing the traditional Welsh fern pattern while the green one has a cord and tassel motif.
(Courtesy of the Museum of Costume, Bath).

Trim the edges of the quilted material

Pin and sew on the binding

Turn the binding to the wrong side of the material and hem

stuffing are inserted between the two layers–a stuffing stick or any blunt instrument such as the end of a crochet hook will serve the purpose. When the area is fully, and even quite tightly, padded the parted threads of the backing are pulled together and secured.

Patterns

Most of the traditional quilting patterns can be adapted for this technique, which is particularly good for adding emphasis to leaves and the petals of flowers, for example.

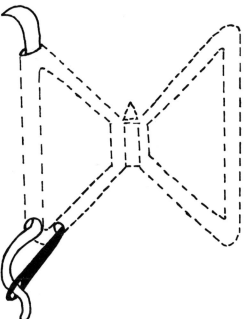

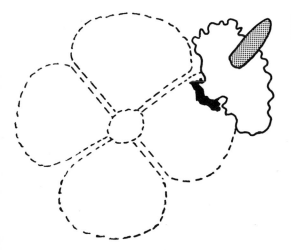

ITALIAN QUILTING
Materials
As for Stuffed Quilting.

Method

The pattern is again worked as for any other type of quilting but this technique is really confined to lines, usually parallel lines that should have as few breaks or intersections as possible. When the design is stitched, a cord, ideally thick soft wool known as Italian quilting wool, is pulled through the channel made by the lines of stitching–this is best done with a tapestry needle. When the lines cross or if there is an abrupt change of angle the wool should be pulled out and then

re-inserted into the same hole. It is advisable to leave a small loop at these points which will prevent puckering and allow for shrinkage. Several lines of Italian Quilting make a very effective border for a cushion cover or any small item.

CONTOUR QUILTING

This type of quilting is best illustrated

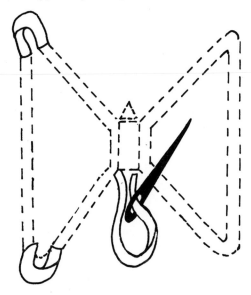

in Hawaiian quilts, its characteristic being that the quilting pattern is determined entirely by the applied design. Rows of running stitches about half an inch apart follow the outline of the appliqué, giving the impression of contour lines on a map. Since the quilting is governed by the overall design it seems appropriate to describe the design technique although this should strictly come in the section on appliqué.

One hundred and fifty years ago a pioneer company of Missionaries sailed from New England to what was then known as the Sandwich Islands. The women took with them their sewing accessories and bags of fabric scraps for patchwork. This they taught in its simplest form to the local inhabitants who, however, had no scraps of their own since their garments were made of bark or 'tapa'. It seemed wasteful to cut new material into small geometric shapes, so a completely new technique evolved.

Instead of cutting the material into separate shapes, a whole length was used in one piece. This was folded and re-folded and then cut just as in a paper cut-out. The material was then opened out and the whole section laid over the foundation, edges were turned under and then sewn as in ordinary appliqué. The resulting design being all of one piece was quite unlike any other appliqué pattern and lent itself to the outline or contour quilting. The designs were always symbolic and usually inspired by the leaves and fruits of Hawaiian plants.

Another characteristic of Hawaiian quilts which has been consistent right through to the present time when they are being made for the tourist trade is the use of bright red – either the foundation or the applied top is nearly always red, usually used with white as in the illustration opposite.

The diagram on page 24 illustrates the method of cutting an applied design.

OTHER FORMS OF QUILTING

There are other forms of quilting beyond the scope of this particular book, usually covered by the general term 'linen quilting'.

Linen quilting uses no wadding as an inner layer, as its purpose is solely for decoration and not for warmth. Here the sewing is often done in silk in back stitch and in monotone. Embroidery is sometimes incorporated into the design. The earliest known example of this type of work is part of a Sicilian Quilt, dated about A.D. 1400 now in the Victoria and Albert Museum. In the 17th and 18th Centuries this form of quilting was used for men's waistcoats, jackets for children and head caps, as well as for coverlets and bed-hangings. The caps were a necessity when houses were so cold and draughty. Most linen quilting is extremely fine and well executed and would therefore be more likely to have been carried out in the homes of the gentry than in the villages.

SIMPLIFIED HAWAIIAN TYPE QUILT

Instructions

Cut a twelve inch square of red material.

Fold in half lengthways, again cross-ways and then diagonally. The material will now be the size of the pattern on page 24.

Pin pattern to folded material and cut on solid lines only.

Open out material, turn in small hem all round and appliqué to background.

Detail of Hawaiian Quilt
The small section shown opposite of a very large Hawaiian Quilt shows outline or contour quilting.

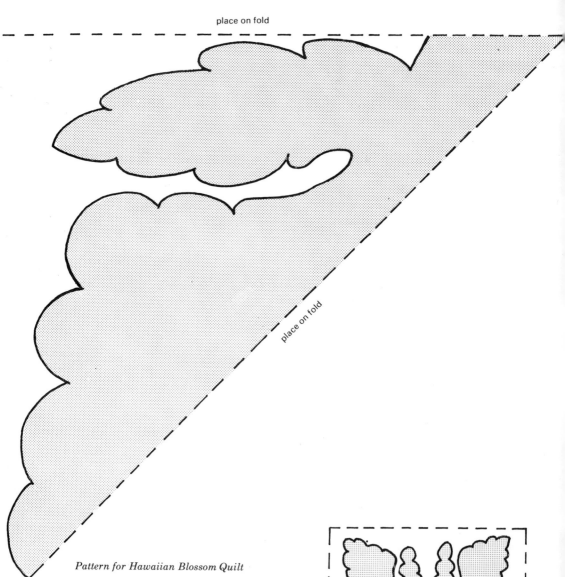

place on fold

place on fold

Pattern for Hawaiian Blossom Quilt

The small diagram can be treated as just one square for making into a block quilt. When the blocks are all joined contour quilting can be carried out over the whole area.

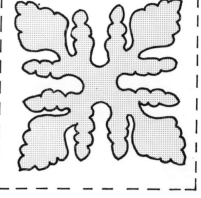

Full pattern when material is unfolded

24

QUILTING PATTERNS

On the following pages there are some suggested patterns for quilting. The patterns are stitched straight on to the material being quilted and do not rely on the use of patchwork and appliqué for effect. In all cases the pattern outlines should be marked on to the material before quilting is begun.

Patterns Based on Straight Lines

These lines are continued in a regular fashion all over the material being quilted.

Square Diamonds

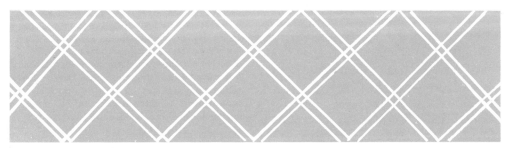

Elongated Diamonds

Double Diamonds

Patterns Based on Circles

There are endless variations of patterns based on circles. Here, and on page 28, are just a few, but you will be able to think of many more. Draw a circle the size you require and mark in the pattern. Many of these will look particularly effective if worked on to material which has a circular motif in the pattern.

Shell

Fan

Star

Rose

Feather Circle

Friendship or Album Quilt

In the field of appliqué this is a very typically American idea – every square is made by a different person who usually signed it. There is no attempt at any unifying theme and the charm of these quilts is more in their interest than in their beauty. An extraordinary variety of subjects can be depicted in any one quilt and the same idea opens up endless possibilities for the needlewoman of today.

(Courtesy of the American Museum in Britain).

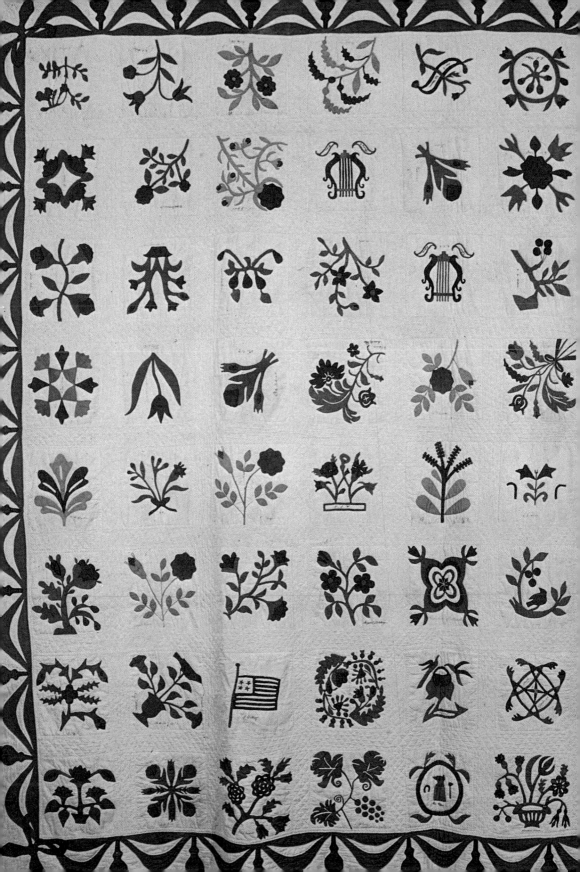

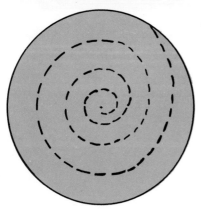

Snail Creep

Wineglass or Teacup

Wineglass or teacup patterns are
produced by combining circles together
for effect. Many different patterns can
be created in this way. Try the ones we
have illustrated.

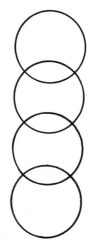

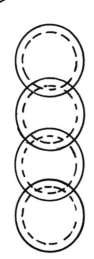

Miscellaneous Designs

Here are a variety of miscellaneous designs which make attractive quilting patterns. Use these as trace-off patterns to make templates remembering to mark the outline only on the material. The dotted lines can then be easily stitched in.

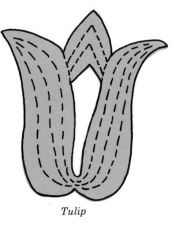

Tulip

Banana

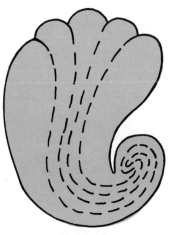

Paisley Pear

Welsh Tulip

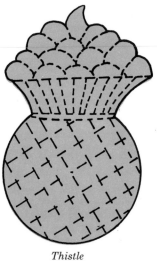

Thistle

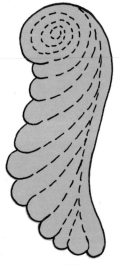

Goose Wing

Paisley Flower

Lined Twist

Cord and Tassel or Hammock

Tenth Anniversary Quilt
Showing modern appliqué at its most imaginative this quilt was made by Mrs Cathleen Maxwell of Bradford-on-Avon, Wilts as a present to her son and daughter-in-law on their tenth wedding anniversary. She has included everything to remind them of their first ten years–their children, their homes, their interests and their cars as well as their respective Saints and items to do with their work and their play. The whole design is held together by the border of linked hexagons and there are the traditional hearts because it is a kind of marriage quilt.

(Courtesy of Mrs Cathleen Maxwell).

History of Patchwork and Appliqué

Patchwork, like quilting, goes back for thousands of years. In ancient Greece, India and China, it was being used centuries before the birth of Christ. It has, in fact, existed ever since cloth has existed and it was born of the need for thrift and economy in the use of this commodity, one of the most valuable known to man. Fragments were saved to be joined together so as to create a new whole, or they were used to repair and strengthen worn garments. From these simple beginnings have grown mosaic patchwork and appliqué, or applied work, as we know them today. Patching in its strictest sense, the application of a section of sound fabric to cover a hole or a worn area, probably came first and in the course of time the patches themselves became decorative. They were used in this way on the Crusaders' banners and in the beautiful ecclesiastical vestments of medieval Europe. From these roots has grown the applied work which is so much a part of modern needlework, especially in the form of 'collage'. As a means of free and creative expression in the contemporary idiom no other branch of the needlewoman's art is so perfectly suited. In America it is still more logically called 'patchwork'. What is now known as mosaic patchwork, or, more usually just 'patchwork' in this country, is 'pieced work' in America, but to save any confusion the English terms will be used in this book. The technique of mosaic patchwork developed from the joining together of small fragments of precious fabric by over-sewing on the wrong side. At first there was no attempt at any pattern, the arrange-ment being governed only by the size of the fragments, but just as patches became decorative so these pieces evolved into regular geometric shapes organised into clearly defined patterns. The fact that all patchwork is based on geometric shapes has meant that it has not changed in essence over the centuries; only the fabrics have changed and the combination of different shapes has increased in complexity. The basic shapes have always been squares, triangles, hexagons and diamonds, the simple but ordered arrangement of which characterized early patchwork and was the basis of all traditional patterns; some of these are shown on page 35. The introduction of more complicated shapes has not necessarily enhanced the beauty of the work, which depends so much on the blending of colour and of the fabrics themselves. The hexagon has probably always been the most widely used shape. It is, in fact, what the bees use in a honeycomb and is certainly the easiest for joining together. Much of the patchwork being done today is concentrated on the many variations by which hexagons can be formed into patterns and the lovely quilt illustrated on page 39 should provide inspiration, while the very easy version on page 51 is an encouragement to beginners.

The most common use for patchwork has always been in the making of bed-covers–a whole quilt and even hangings for a four-poster bed could be made from scraps and was, therefore, the 'something out of nothing' that appealed so strongly in the days when cloth was scarce and expensive. It is this aspect of thrift that has given patchwork its particular character, more 'grass-roots' than other forms of needlework, and as such it has reflected the life and the taste of ordinary people. Patchwork was made from pieces saved from worn garments or from when these garments were cut out –unsophisticated fabrics such as homespun linens, and the 'painted calicoes' and 'chints' that were imported so cheaply from India in the 17th Century. It was only much later that material was actually bought for making into patchwork and it has always been in the use of simple everyday materials that it has been most successful. Although used in Victorian times, silks, satins and velvets have never had the same charm, apart from which they do not wash or stand the test of time.

In the story of quilt-making, patchwork and appliqué have developed together, applied work tending to be more popular in America, and many of the most beautiful quilts that have survived are a combination of both techniques with quilting as well. Patchwork by itself is abstract and can only suggest motifs whereas there is no limit as to what can be interpreted in appliqué. Not being governed by the same discipline, appliqué patterns have never shown the same traditional consistency, so that the old descriptive names apply mostly to pure patchwork. Although these patterns may not have changed for hundreds of years the overall appearance of quilts have altered because dress materials have been the primary source for patchwork and the changing face of fashion has brought radical differences in colour and texture. For this reason it provides a rich field for students of costume and textile design–the 'Log Cabin' quilt on page 43 is a particularly good example of this.

Some of the oldest traditional patterns, however, when only a single colour was combined with white, are among the most attractive and these, interpreted in modern fabrics, look much as they did two hundred years ago. In appliqué there was a fashion in the closing years of the 18th Century for using the beautiful copper-plate chintzes so popular for furnishings. These chintzes were too expensive to permit their use for whole quilts so that particular motifs were carefully cut out and appliquéd to a plain background, usually unbleached calico–a technique demanding great accuracy and patience. More generally appliqué has been in the field of free expression, in artistic terms being almost a substitute for painting. In the later years of the 19th Century the rendering of flowers, foliage, birds, patriotic emblems or religious symbols, anything in fact that took the maker's fancy, ran riot with results that were not always successful. In the present revival of quilt-making, appliqué has reverted to far greater simplicity with bold motifs and clear outlines, demanding less skill in the sewing but giving back something of the vigour and freshness of the early work–the modern quilts shown on pages 11 and 31 bear this out.

Although traditional patterns both in patchwork and appliqué were taken from England to America by the early colonists it was there, inspired perhaps by the even greater need for economy in the use of cloth, that the making of quilts assumed a greater importance than in any other country. For this reason and because the reverse process is now in operation with the inspiration spreading back from America to this country, it seems logical to talk of patchwork in America first.

From 1750 until 1850 it flourished to an extraordinary and universal extent so that women everywhere threw

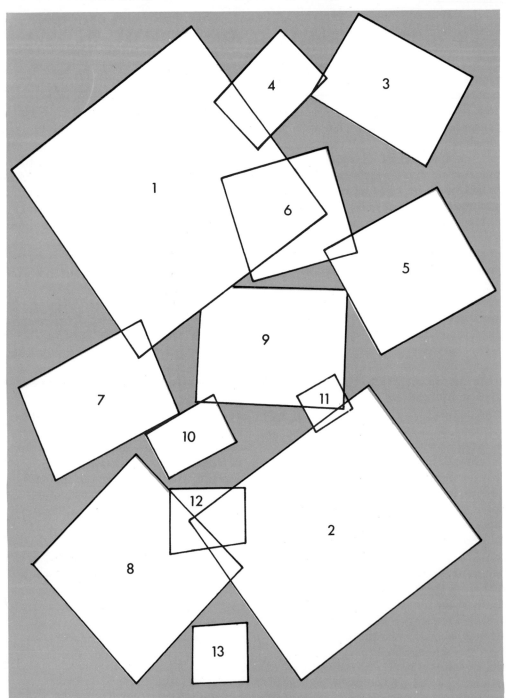

Patchwork Patterns

These samples of traditional patchwork patterns shown overleaf include most of the popular ones that were used in quilts both in this country and America in the 19th Century. They have been made by Mrs Shiela Betterton and are used when she lectures on American needlework.

1. Double Wedding Ring, 2. Double Irish Chain, 3. Tumbling Blocks, 4. Turkey Tracks, 5. Honey Bee, 6. Bird in the Window, 7. Goose Tracks, 8. Lancaster County Rose, 9. Mosaic, 10. Log Cabin, 11. 4-Patch, 12. 9-Patch, 13. Saw Tooth.

themselves into the making of patchwork quilts with passionate enthusiasm, perhaps because it was the only way in which they could satisfy their hunger for colour and decoration in homes that enjoyed few other refinements. At first with their own homespun linens and later when imported calicoes and chintzes were available women and girls, even in the most remote places and difficult conditions, cut and sewed their patches, met together at Quilting Bees and produced coverlets of extraordinary beauty, thus contributing to the folk art culture that is so uniquely American. When it is remembered that girls were supposed to start married life owning at least twelve quilts the tremendous output can be imagined and this has happily ensured the survival of a rich legacy even to this day. In homes all over the country women continue to treasure, often to use, the quilts made by their grandmothers and great-grandmothers. It is only fairly recently, however, that many of these old quilts have found their way into museum collections and into exhibitions that draw thousands of admiring viewers.

Something of the romance, even the mystique, of American patchwork is reflected in the names of traditional patterns, names drawn from the experiences of everyday life but showing a vividness of imagination that had nothing to do with education or artistic training. 'Log Cabin', 'Barn Raising', 'Prairie Lily', 'Bear's Paw', 'Prickly Pear', 'Indian Hatchet', 'Duck's Foot-in-the-Mud', 'Corn and Beans', are just a random selection. Another chapter in the story is told by others – 'The Slave Chain', 'Kansas Troubles', 'Texas Tears', 'Rocky Road to California', 'Delectable Mountains' and sometimes names changed with the great migration westwards so that the 'Ship's Wheel' of Cape Cod became 'Harvest Sun' in the Mid-West.

Many American quilts were made in blocks or squares, a method that simplified the sewing and made for speed in that several people could work on a quilt at the same time, their respective portions being joined into the overall design later. An adaptation of this technique was in the 'Album' or 'Friendship' quilts using appliqué motifs with each square being made by a different person who usually signed, and sometimes dated it, using Indian ink. The extraordinary variety of motifs combined in a quilt of this kind made for interest rather than beauty – a very characteristic Album Quilt can be seen on page 27.

The earliest known patchwork in England was made at Levens Hall in Westmorland in 1708 and can still be seen there. It is a remarkable piece of work, a quilt and bed-hangings, made of imported Indian calicoes in shades of red and blue, some of the patches being themselves made up of small fragments of the more rare fabrics, and the whole area being quilted in a diamond pattern. Few other examples of patchwork quilts made before the last years of the 18th Century have survived, which is hardly surprising since they were made for hard and instant use and not as works of art.

Although never achieving quite the same significance as in America there was a craze for patchwork in the early years of the 19th Century in this country. Printed cottons were by then very cheap – two shillings a yard – and even 'new painted chintzes' were little more. Manufacturers actually produced specially printed panels for use as centre pieces and these often commemorated national events such as Nelson's and Wellington's victories or the marriage of Princess Charlotte, and chintz borders were also printed to match the panels, a sophistication not enjoyed in America. Although primarily a cottage activity patchwork was also undertaken by the ladies of the big houses using richer fabrics and more sophisticated designs but, handsome as the results often were, they lacked something of the true character of the craft. A link, however, was maintained between the big house and the cottage in that village dressmakers, or the girls who worked as servants in the big houses and salvaged scraps from their mistresses' dresses, were a recognised source for providing pieces so that expensive fabrics did find their way into ordinary country patchwork. Another common source was found in the patterns issued by trade houses to drapers' and tailors' shops – whole quilts were sometimes made with small samples of shirtings, even tickings. Until quite recently factories have sold off very cheaply short lengths and remnants known as 'fents' – these were often sold by weight and sometimes bundles were done up to be sold for as little as one penny.

From the beginning of this century patchwork almost completely died out in England and it is only quite recently that it has regained its popularity, coming like so much else from across the Atlantic. Although being taken up in private homes and by Women's Institutes and Townswomen's Guilds all over the country it is still not nearly so widely practised as in America. There are various short-cuts now available in that templates for patchwork and appliqué are sold in most needlework shops; there are even 'packs' with material and instructions already prepared. This may be an advantage for beginners but does detract from the essential character of patchwork which should be above all an individual expression both in the design itself and in the fabrics used.

One of the greatest advantages of patchwork in the busy life of today is that it can be so easily taken up and put down, and can even be reconciled with watching, or half-watching, television! This is specially the case if the American system of making a quilt as a series of blocks to be joined at a later stage is adopted. In the following pages old patchwork and appliqué patterns are illustrated and since these have never been surpassed in beauty they may provide the inspiration, but it will also be shown how old techniques and designs can be effectively translated into modern terms.

Patchwork

MATERIALS

The materials used should be firm and non-stretch and of the same thickness in any one piece of work. Very well-worn material should be avoided and if old and new are to be used in the same item the new should be washed first. The size of the finished article and the thickness of the material should be taken into account when deciding the size of individual patches. The first available sewing cotton, 60 or even 100, should be used or the new polyester thread is excellent–it is best to use white for all pale colours and black for the dark. When joining dark colours to white a dark thread is less noticeable. As fine a needle as possible should be used.

The pattern shapes called 'templates' are best made of metal or plastic–these can now be bought in all shapes and sizes. From these the papers are cut– old documents or thick brown wrapping paper are best and it is very important that they should be cut with great accuracy.

METHOD OF WORKING

As templates can now be bought in different sizes the easiest method is to work with two of the same shape, one being a quarter inch larger than the other. The smaller is used for cutting the papers, the larger for the material. A template in perspex is ideal for cutting the material since it enables exact motifs to be selected from patterned fabrics. This is known as a 'window template'. It is advisable to pencil lightly round the template before cutting the material.

A paper template is laid on the wrong side of the fabric patch, the edges are then turned over and tacked down–special care is needed to secure the corners neatly, most particularly when diamonds and triangles are being used. These shapes are then joined together by over-sewing edge to edge on the wrong side–it is advisable to avoid stitching through the papers so that these can be easily removed. By cutting the tacking stitches they can be pulled out and often used again. It is especially important to make sure that all corners match exactly.

Whatever patchwork pattern is chosen it is a good idea to prepare several patches before starting to join them into the requisite arrangements. When planning a design it is helpful to have a soft board or a piece of polystyrene, even a cork bathmat on which the patches can be pinned and moved about. In planning a quilt the patches can be pinned onto an old sheet, and it is advisable to divide the whole area into sections. These sections can be completed one at a time before joining them all together in the final stage. When this has been achieved the result is a 'top'. This is then ready for lining with a plain material, unbleached

---

Mosaic Patchwork
Showing a very sophisticated use of hexagons this beautiful mosaic patchwork quilt was made on a plantation in Virginia during the Civil War. Not only are the hexagons arranged to form diamond units but these diamonds are themselves arranged into box formations. This elaborate arrangement of hexagons is more typically American than British. In this case each patch is outlined in the quilting which forms a very pleasing pattern on the reverse side.
(Courtesy of the American Museum in Britain).

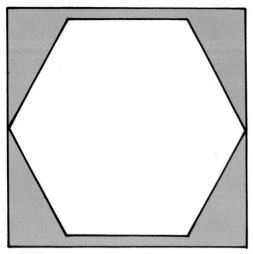

Solid template made from plastic, card or paper

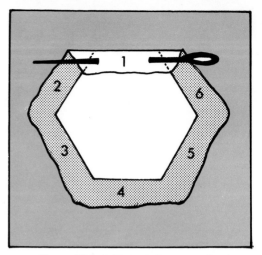

Excess Material is turned over template

calico is the ideal, and the two layers, or three if it is to be padded, are joined together. The two methods for this process are quilting or 'tying'. With both methods the top should be firmly tacked to the backing–this is best achieved by spreading the work on a large table, the floor, or even a bed. Tacking stitches should be done in parallel lines starting always from the same side to prevent wrinkling.

The 'tying' technique consists of making back-stitches at regular intervals using a strong thread and working from the wrong side–two stitches of about one-eighth of an inch in length are all that is necessary. When making the first stitch an end should be left–draw the thread through all layers firmly but without puckering the surface and then cut the thread leaving sufficient length to tie the two

'Window' template made from clear perspex

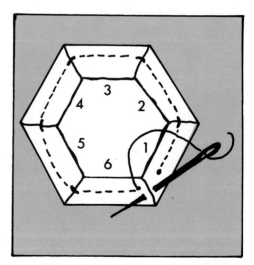

Material is tacked securely in position

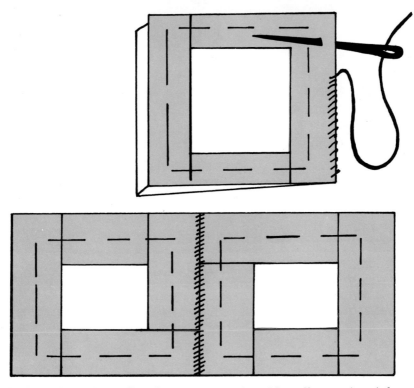

Patches with templates still in place are sewn together with small oversewing stitches

ends in a double reef-knot. Finish by cutting both ends, leaving about one-third of an inch. By choosing strategic points in the pattern and using self-coloured thread these ties are almost invisible on the right side.

FINISHING

There are various methods, the easiest being to cut the top and the backing to match exactly and then binding to make a neat edge. This can pick out one of the colours in the patchwork design. Alternatively both edges can be turned in and a piping cord inserted. Still another method is to leave the top about one and a half inches larger than the lining and then turn it over and hem it to the lining on the wrong side. Braid or fringe can be added to give an extra finish.

SIMPLE PATCHWORK PATTERNS

Squares, triangles, diamonds and hexagons are the most commonly used patchwork shapes, with hexagons perhaps the most popular of all. All these shapes can be used to form designs on their own or they can be combined with one another. The mixing of colours is very important in patchwork and magnificent designs can be achieved by clever and subtle colour placing. Designs and patchwork combinations are shown on the following pages.

Squares and Triangles

Each of the patterns illustrated on page 42 could be used as a block in making a quilt and are most effective when alternated with plain blocks of equal size.

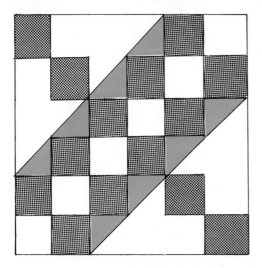
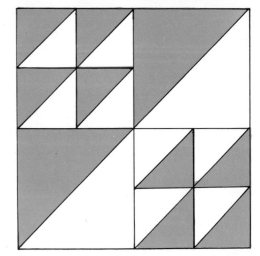
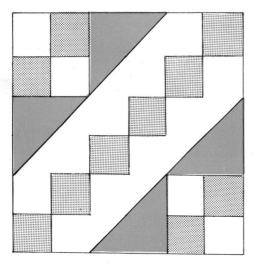
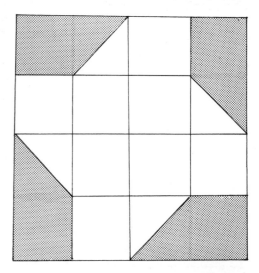
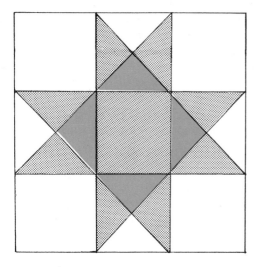
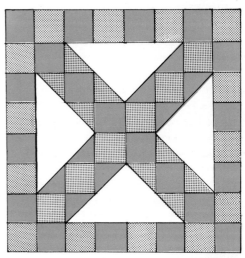

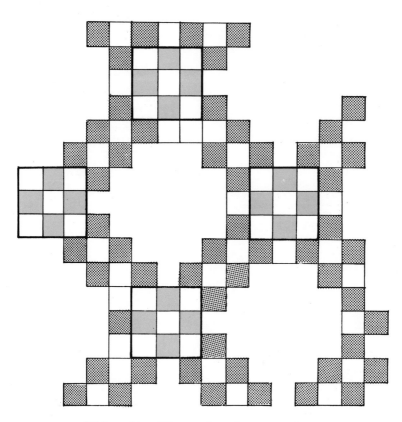

*White and two different coloured squares make up
this pattern which is often used in quilt-making*

Log Cabin

Like the 'Double Wedding Ring' shown on page
63 this is not an easy pattern but one which
challenges the skill of an experienced needlewoman who has a good sense of colour and a
large supply of scraps in dark and light shades. It
is one of the most popular of all American quilt
patterns in applied work. This particular Log
Cabin shows a rather subtle use of muted colours
all perfectly balanced. Instructions for making
this quilt will be found on page 57.

(Courtesy of the American Museum in Britain).

Hexagons

Hexagons can be combined together in
rosettes (see diagrams 1 and 2), in
diamond shapes (diagram 3) or in
stripes (diagrams 4, 5 and 6), but again
all these effects are achieved by clever
colour positioning of the different
patches. They can also be used to make
attractive borders (diagram 7).
Hexagons can be of any size from 1 in
(each side) to 3 in.

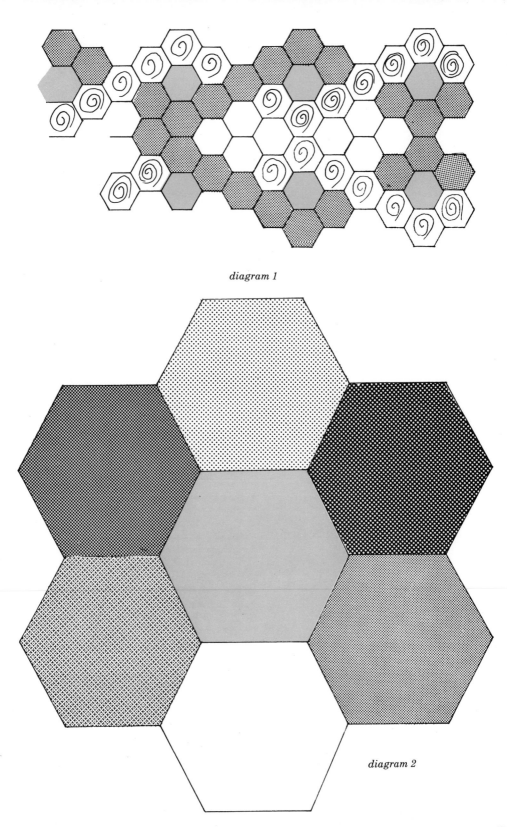

diagram 1

diagram 2

45

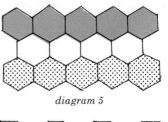

diagram 5

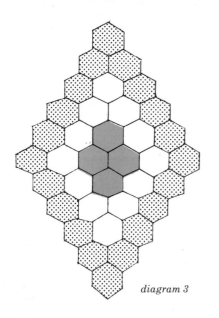

diagram 3

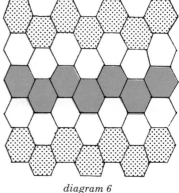

diagram 6

Star

One of the most popular uses for diamond patches was in the creation of Star Motifs. These occur over and over again in American quilts, sometimes called 'Star of Bethlehem', sometimes 'Sunburst'. The beauty of this particular star lies in the choice of printed fabrics. Built up from a central eight-point star each layer of diamond patches is in a different print beautifully matched. The shading of each layer blends into the next with extraordinary artistry and it is this which gives the impression of such intricacy.

This is a late 19th Century American quilt with thicker than usual padding which, combined with its smaller than usual size, only 5 ft 4 ins × 6 ft, suggests that it was intended more in the nature of an eiderdown than a coverlet. The graceful curves of the quilted feather border are in happy contrast to the angles of the star.

(Courtesy of the American Museum in Britain).

diagram 4

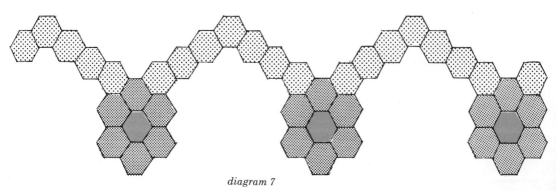

diagram 7

Diamonds

Diamond templates have been used here to make six and eight-point stars. The eight-point star has been finished off with square and triangular shapes to make a complete square block, which would be most effective used in an overall pattern to make a quilt. Diamond stars are the basis of many traditional patterns.

Diamonds are particularly difficult to cut accurately so that they fit together perfectly, so extra care should be taken when working with diamond shapes.

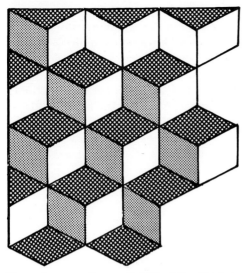

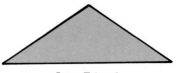

Long Triangle

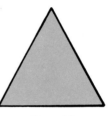

Pyramid

Box pattern sometimes called 'Tumbling Blocks'. This pattern is most effective when carried out in diamonds of three shades of which one must be dark.

Some Other Shapes

Here, and on page 50, are some more shapes that can be used in patchwork patterns. They can be combined with squares and hexagons and used in any number of ways.

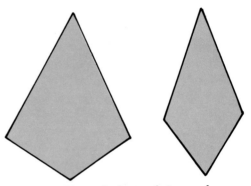

Diamonds shortened at one end

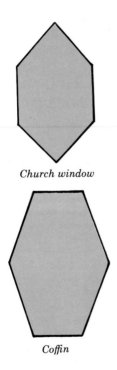

Church window

Coffin

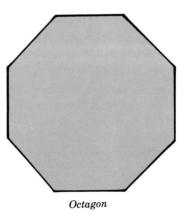

Octagon

Pentagon 1

Pentagon 2

SIMPLE MOSAIC PATCHWORK

Materials
Coloured poplin blocks for top.
Scraps of cotton prints and poplins for
   hexagonal motifs.
Calico for backing.
Polyester wadding for filling.
(This quilt will wash easily and drip-
dry).

Instructions
Cut sufficient 10 inch squares of poplin
to cover top of bed. Make up hexagonal
motifs as shown on page 45.
Remove papers and appliqué motifs to
blocks making sure that they are
exactly in the centre. Leave some
blocks plain.

Join all the blocks together
alternating plain and motif blocks.
Feather stitch round each block either
on the seams or within the block.
Attach filling and backing and quilt
with a simple pattern, perhaps with a
pattern accentuating the hexagonal
design as in the one in the photograph.
(This quilt can be fitted to a valance if
required or extended to be a whole
coverlet).

SIMPLE PATCHWORK DESIGN APPLIQUED TO FOUNDATION

These are both designs for one block of
a whole quilt. In each case the motif is
made of patchwork and it is then
applied to the foundation as in the quilt
illustrated opposite.

Basket Triangles (shown overleaf)
A very popular traditional pattern.
The basket is usually depicted in red.
The handle also in red is an applied
strip. Each basket is set in a square
block and the blocks can be arranged
in a variety of ways. Quilting stitches
are worked round the edge of the
handle and the seams of the triangles.
Background areas can be quilted in a
decorative design such as a leaf motif.

Simple Mosaic Patchwork
For anyone new to the art of patchwork and
wanting the encouragement of quick results this
is an ideal example. Rosettes made up of
hexagons are appliquéd to foundation squares
which are then joined.
This quilt made in the form of a fitted divan
cover is the work of Mrs Shiela Betterton,
using scraps from her own and her daughter's
dresses. There is no need for any matching of
printed patterns in the hexagons so that any
number of different fabric pieces can be used.
(Courtesy of Mrs Shiela Betterton).

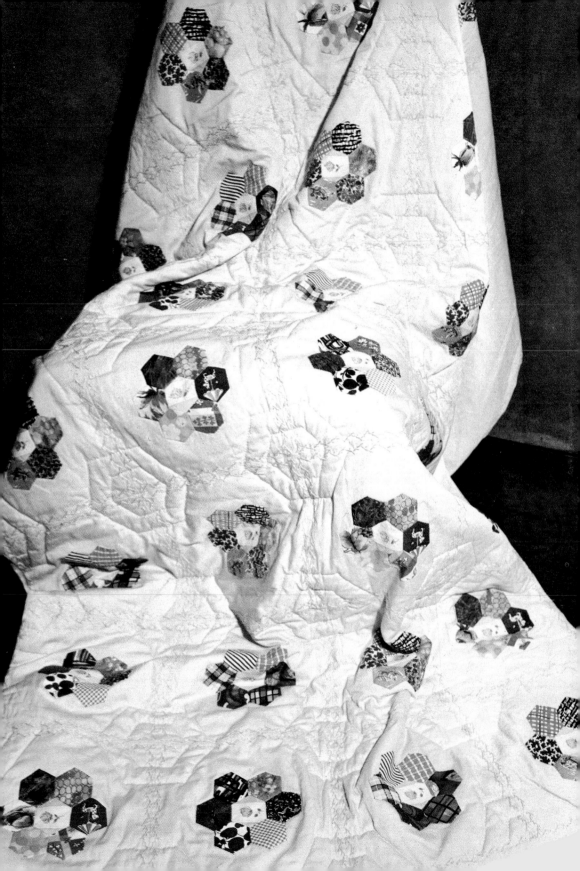

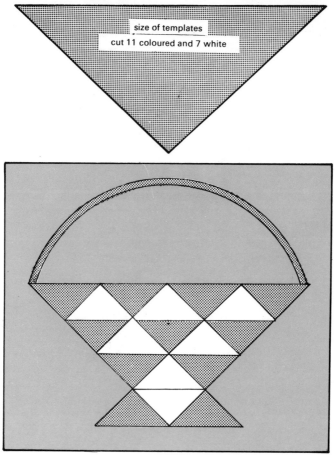

Basket Triangles

North Carolina Lily

Another traditional block pattern – the lilies are set in diagonal blocks and the leaves and stems are in appliqué. Again quilting is done round the outlines and the design can be repeated in quilting stitches in the plain areas of the quilt.

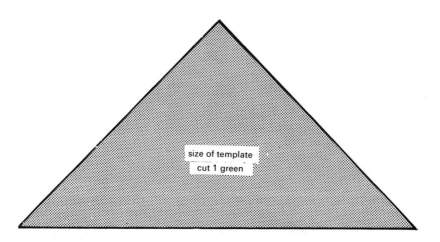

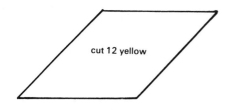

cut 12 yellow

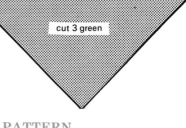

cut 3 green

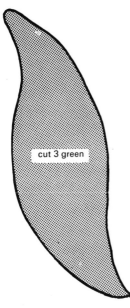

cut 3 green

STAR PATTERN

The foundation for this Star pattern quilt is an eight-point star. Traditionally this should be in a plain fabric. It is then surrounded by diamond patches of a contrasting shade. The next layer of diamond patches is again different – this process of adding ever widening layers is continued until the required size is attained.

The final layer is effective if a strong colour tone is used to give a clearly defined outline. In the traditional 'Star of Bethlehem' pattern the points of the star are extended so that the completed unit is in itself a large eight-point star. For this pattern it is essential to make sure that there is sufficient fabric to complete each layer. Because of this it is not a recommended pattern for 'scraps' – certainly for the large outer layers it is necessary to buy material.

North Carolina Lily

Each layer of the star is marked in diamonds of the same material.

53

MOSAIC DIAMOND

A Mosaic Diamond effect can be
achieved from placing hexagons
together as shown in Diagram 1.
Each Mosaic Diamond is surrounded by
hexagons of a plain colour. And as in

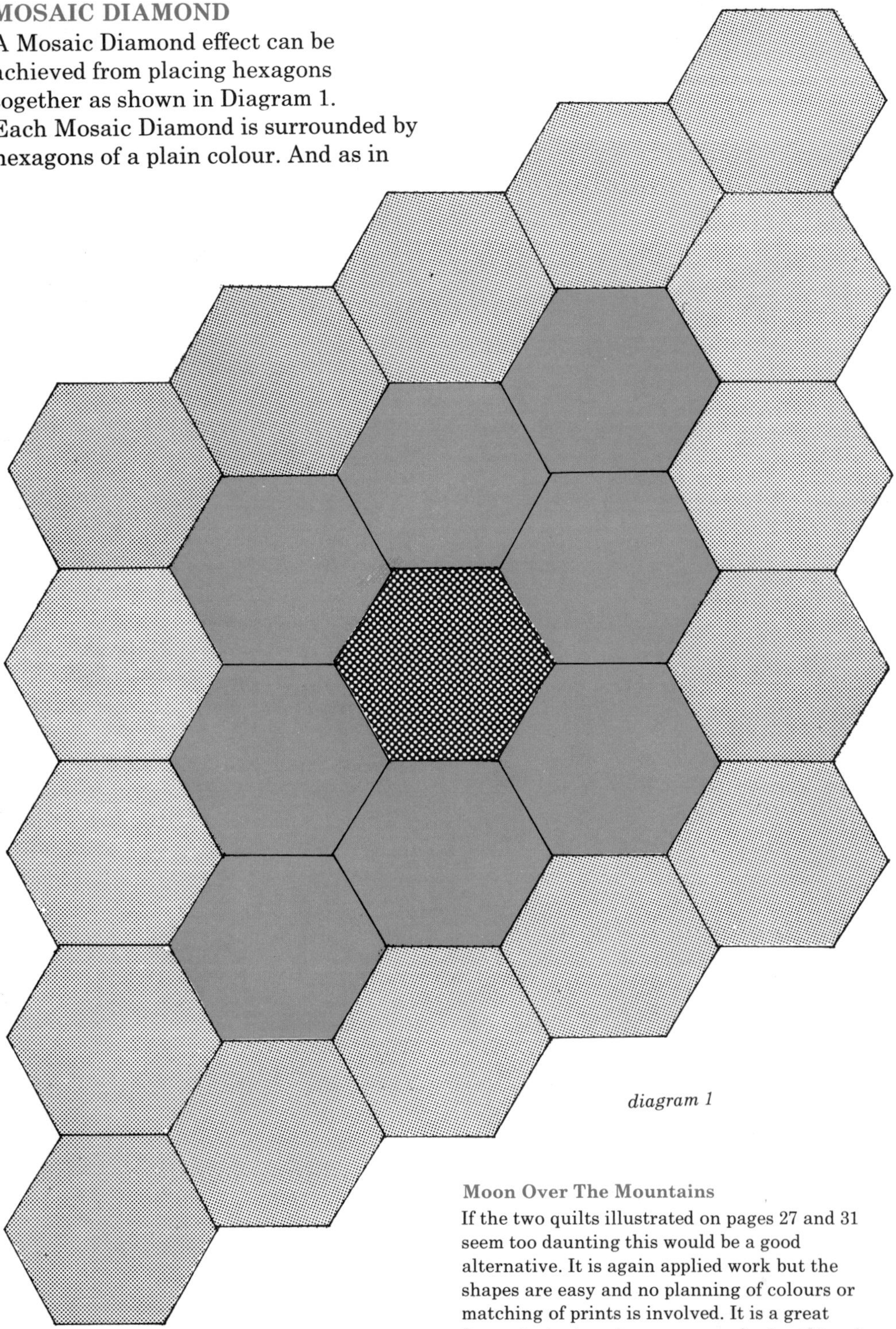

diagram 1

Moon Over The Mountains

If the two quilts illustrated on pages 27 and 31
seem too daunting this would be a good
alternative. It is again applied work but the
shapes are easy and no planning of colours or
matching of prints is involved. It is a great
favourite in America among professional teachers
of needlework as a first exercise in quilt making.

(Courtesy of Mrs Shiela Betterton).

the beautiful quilt illustrated on page 39, a patch in a strong colour should be used uniformly at the intersections of the plain border. Diagram 2 shows the lay-out of hexagons used in such a quilt.

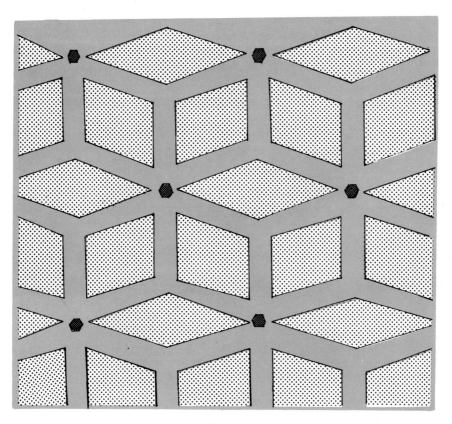

diagram 2

LOG CABIN PATTERN CUSHION COVER

To make a traditional 'Log Cabin'-pattern cushion cover you will need the following:
For each block:
10 in square of calico to be used as foundation.
One 2 in square of plain coloured material.

An equal number of dark and light strips of material/ribbon 1 inch wide. The lengths of the strips will vary according to their position in the dock. Four blocks joined together will make a cushion cover. Diagram 5 has some suggestions for joining the blocks together.

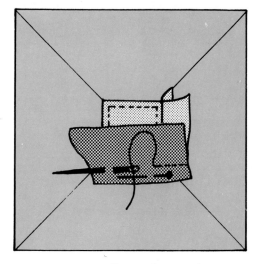

diagram 1

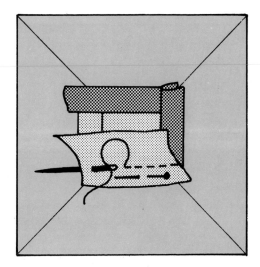

diagram 3

Instructions

Crease foundation block to mark centre.

Tack 2 in square of material to foundation block matching centres (diagram 1).

Cut two strips of light material and two strips of dark a little longer than the square.

Place edge of one strip of light material to edge of square right sides facing, overlapping about half an inch each end, and sew down one eighth of an inch from edge (diagram 2).

Fold strip over to show right side and press.

Repeat with second light strip on an adjoining side of the square, overlapping end of first strip (diagram 3).

In the same manner, sew dark

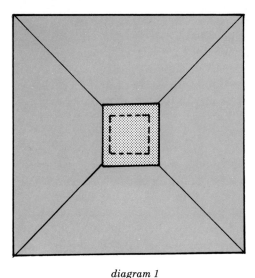

diagram 2

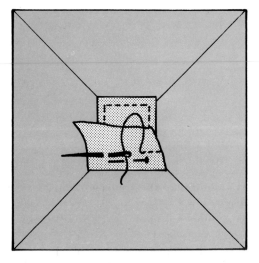

diagram 4

diagram 5

strips on remaining two sides (diagram 4).

Repeat the process with four longer strips, overlapping ends of the previous row by about half an inch. Continue in this way until five rows of 'logs' have been laid. The edge of the last row should meet the edge of the foundation block.

The blocks are then joined together by sewing firmly on the wrong side. Attach plain backing of similar size. The proportions of the centre square and strips can be varied but light strips are always placed on one side and dark on the other.

To complete, quilt along the seams between the patches. A special quilting design is not needed for this pattern.

MOON OVER THE MOUNTAINS

The 'Moon over the Mountain' is a fine example of a 'three patch pattern' used in quilt making. It is not too difficult to work but extremely effective when complete, as can be seen from the photograph on p. 55. Use the patterns drawn in the diagram to make templates. The instructions we have given make a coverlet approximately 80 × 100 ins with each block measuring approximately 8 ins.

Materials

2½ yards white.
4 yards blue sprigged to represent the 'Milky Way'.
2 yards dark blue poplin.
1 yard yellow or gold poplin.
7 yards calico for backing.
(This coverlet has no wadding.)

Instructions
From white material cut 49 blocks each 9 ins square.

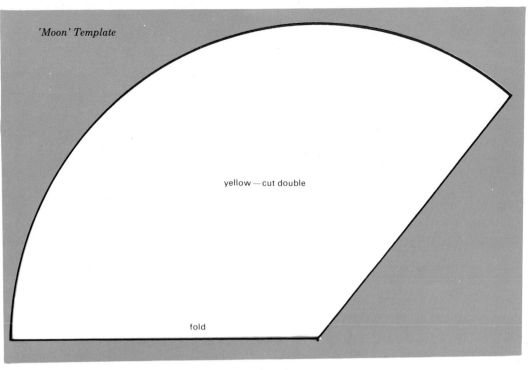

'Moon' Template

yellow — cut double

fold

size of templates

From blue sprigged material cut 50 blocks each 9 ins square.
Cut 49 moons from yellow poplin and 49 mountains from dark blue poplin. Hem blue mountains and yellow moons to the blue sprigged blocks. Join worked blocks to plain white blocks alternately as shown in diagram 1.

From left over material cut strips of plain blue and patterned blue material 3 ins wide and long enough to go completely round the coverlet. Join strips to edge of blocks, inner strip of sprigged material and outer strip of plain blue (diagram 1). Cut and join calico backing to fit top and tack the two layers firmly together. (It will probably be wise to lay them out on the floor.)

a simple pattern, perhaps the outline of the moon over the mountain (diagram 1).
The edges are turned in and finished with two rows of running stitch.

Moon over the Mountain
diagram 1

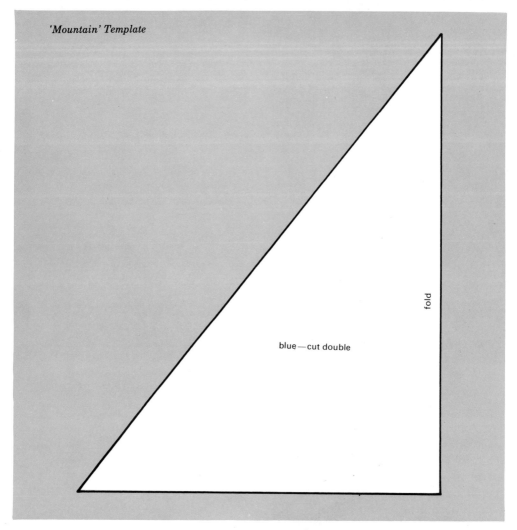

'Mountain' Template

blue—cut double

fold

size of templates

GOOSE TRACKS

This is another very attractive simple patchwork design you might like to try. As a quilt pattern is most effective if carried out in one plain colour with white. Each block is entirely made up of pieced work.

Using the templates opposite and on page 62, cut out the appropriate number of patches from blue and white material as indicated. Join together to make the pattern shown in the block here. Make several identical blocks and join together, alternating with plain blocks if you like. Make into a quilt in the usual way.

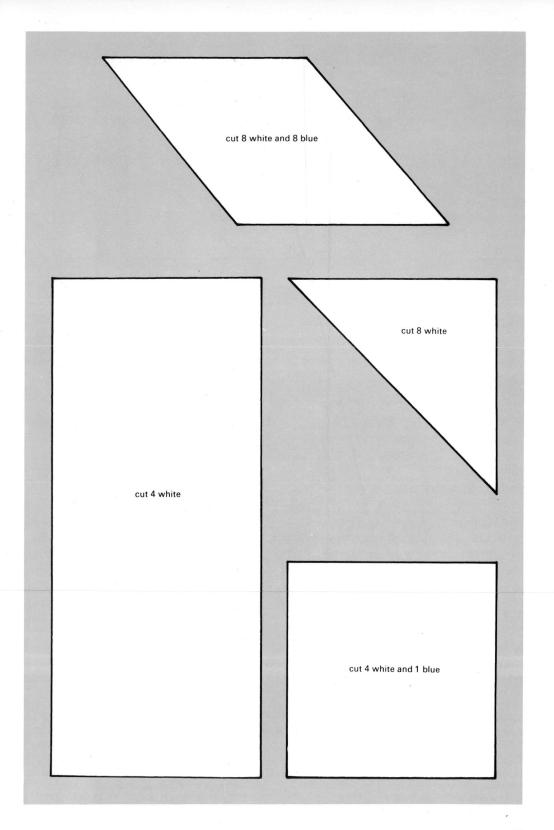

cut 8 white and 8 blue

cut 8 white

cut 4 white

cut 4 white and 1 blue

DOUBLE WEDDING RING

The Double Wedding Ring pattern is a little more complicated than some to work, but makes a most attractive quilt. Each unit consists of eight squares of variegated fabric sewn together to form an arc, with a blue square or a pink square at one end. (Of course this choice of colour is arbitrary, but it is a good idea to choose strong and contrasting colours.) The units are built up as shown in diagram 1. Then two units are joined together to form an oval and a white oval shape is inserted. Units are then assembled as in diagram 2. The star-like centre can be pieced in, or for easier working, the units of coloured fabric can be appliquéd on to a white backing. Simple diagonal quilting should be worked over the white background.

Double Wedding Ring
Not for beginners but showing what can be achieved with practice and skill this is a modern version of a very well loved American design. This pattern is patchwork and allows for the use of any number of different fabric pieces. Traditionally only the four square patches at the intersection of the circles need to be in uniform colours throughout, and again traditionally these are always in a plain material while the pieces are in prints. This quilt was made in Clarksville, Texas in 1930 by Mrs Grace Muns Chain, using scraps saved over many years from her daughter's dresses. It is quilted all over in a pattern that roughly follows the patchwork.
(Courtesy of the American Museum in Britain).

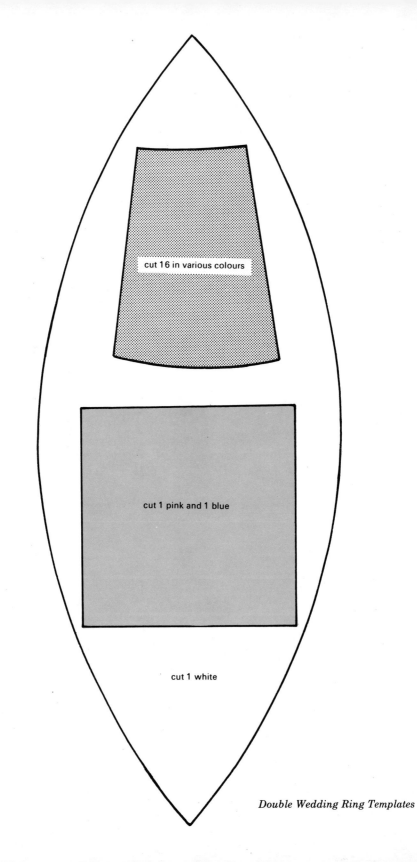

cut 16 in various colours

cut 1 pink and 1 blue

cut 1 white

Double Wedding Ring Templates

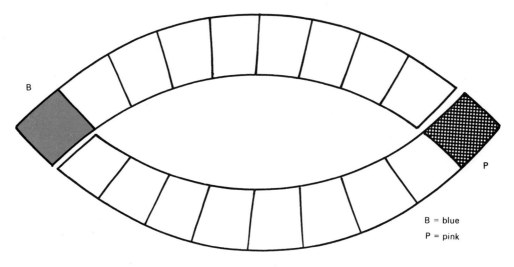

B = blue
P = pink

diagram 1

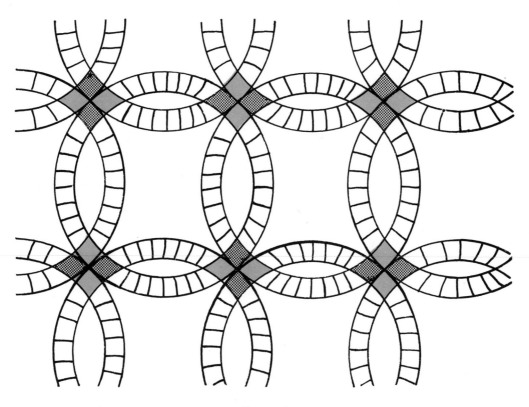

diagram 2

Appliqué

There are few rules for appliqué–this is where imagination comes in. Almost anything with a good clear outline can be translated in appliqué. Some materials are better than others and on the whole man-made fabrics are not as good as the natural ones–anything that obviously frays should be avoided and, as with patchwork, the thicknesses of the materials should be as nearly matched as possible. The ideal foundation material is unbleached calico but this does need to be washed first.

INSTRUCTIONS

To take advantage of modern materials an easy, if unorthodox, method is to use vilene (iron-on stiffening) for the templates, and these become incorporated into the work–the thinnest quality of vilene available with an adhesive backing is the best. With very simple motifs it may be possible to draw or trace straight onto the vilene, remembering to do so on the non-sticky side. With any complex motif it is better to use a paper pattern for cutting the vilene. If the subject to be applied is made up of component parts that need to be cut out separately it is advisable to make two drawings–one on stiff paper to be cut up and the other to keep as a guide for when the parts are re-assembled.

When the vilene has been cut into the required shape it is secured to the fabric using a hot iron, again remembering to put the sticky side of the vilene against the wrong side of the material. The material can now be cut round the vilene shape leaving sufficient for turnings which should be tacked or pressed down. The shape is now ready to be applied to the foundation; it should be tacked or pinned into position first. Small hemming stitches are the best although some people prefer to use a slip-stitch or 'blind' stitch–traditionally, however, stitches are not supposed to be invisible, only regular and as small as possible. It is advisable to use thread in the same colour as the applied motif, fine cotton or polyester thread being the best. The vilene template gives a beautifully firm tailored outline and being washable it is ideal for all appliqué.

Embroidery, even of the simplest kind such as stem-stitch or chain-stitch, is an almost essential feature for picking out detail–for the stalks of flowers and leaves, for marking the overlap of petals and for the centres of flowers, for wings and beaks of birds, for details on houses, in fact for any sharp points. Even shading can be achieved with a little simple embroidery and this gives depth and realism to many objects that would otherwise be flat and featureless.

Birds of Paradise
Birds of Paradise were a very popular subject in America in the middle years of the 19th Century and the illustration opposite is an unusually sophisticated rendering of them showing great technical skill and artistry. No two birds are the same. Like so many American quilts this one is predominantly in red and green. Any keen bird lover who happened also to be an experienced needlewoman might try copying this theme– good clear illustrations of birds might be traced and then translated into templates for appliqué. Leaves or branches could be added and there might be scope for simple embroidery to give the finishing touches.
(Courtesy of the American Museum in Britain).

APPLIQUE PATTERNS

A very popular use of applique in quilting is to make the traditional friendship or album quilts and marriage and anniversary quilts referred to previously and illustrated on pages 11, 27 and 31. You could have great fun devising and making one of these for a friend or relative. Full instructions for making a personalised wedding quilt are given on pages 80 and 81, but here are some more suggestions for motifs.

Appliqué Rose

These pieces combine together to make a most attractive rose as can be seen from the diagram opposite. Use these patterns to trace your templates, but allow turnings on each one. Tack the turnings before applying the pieces onto the quilt or cover.

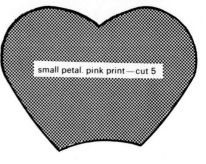

small petal. pink print — cut 5

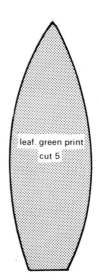

leaf. green print cut 5

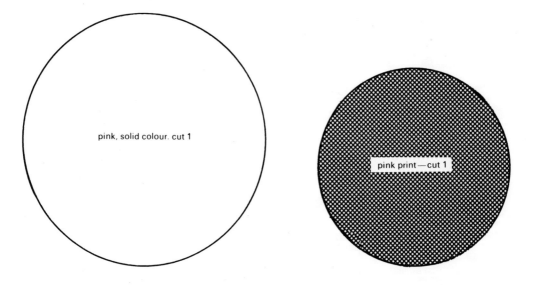

pink, solid colour. cut 1

pink print — cut 1

large petal. pink solid colour — cut 5

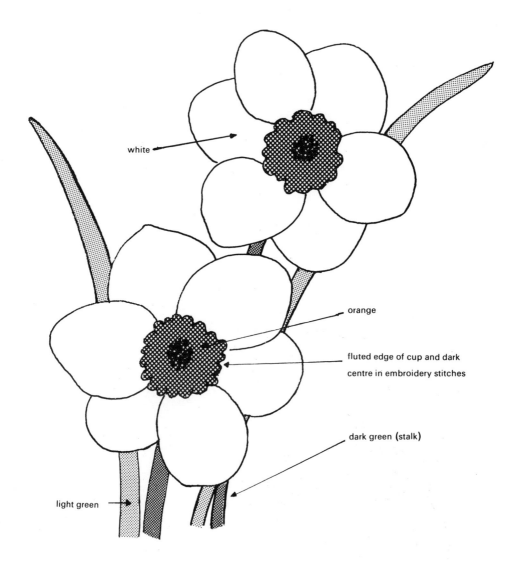

white

orange

fluted edge of cup and dark
centre in embroidery stitches

dark green (stalk)

light green

Narcissi

This design could be very effective
carried out in white on a coloured
background.
In the design the flower petals need
not be cut separately, instead the whole
flower can be treated in outline. The
petals are defined in stem-stitch done in
a slightly deeper shade. The orange cup
is superimposed over the white petals.
If used in a quilt, this motif can be
reversed in alternate blocks so that the
pointed leaves make an arch. Quilt
round the outlines.

Birds

Make birds in different colours and appliqué to a white background
Use embroidery stitches to pick out wing markings, eyes, legs and beaks and the branches can be in patches or suggested in stitches.

Butterflies

These can be in any number of colours on a white background. The basic shapes can be arranged in any pattern. They can be self coloured or the wings can be in different colours. Again, each shape can be treated in one piece and the wings marked with stitching or alternately the wings can be separate patches. The antennae are best done in fine stitching in black and the bodies in satin stitch.

Houses

The roof, side and front are different coloured patches. Stitch in doors, windows and other details in embroidery.

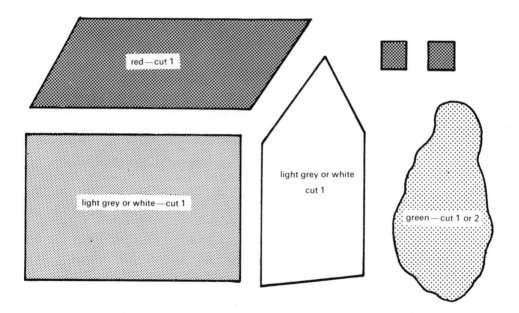

red — cut 1

light grey or white — cut 1

light grey or white
cut 1

green — cut 1 or 2

Useful Hints

Patchwork and appliqué are fascinating and can be done with very little expense. Collect all the material you can from dressmaking, etc., sort it into colours and put each colour into separate plastic bags. You can then see at a glance what you need from any bag. Never throw away the smallest piece as it may be useful sometimes. Don't expect to make a beautiful patchwork design without having to buy some new materials to help.

Too many patterned pieces make a confused design. It is much better to use more plain than patterned pieces.

If you have a piece of material that you really like, study it, and then decide what colours to use with it. For example, if you have a material of blue and purple flowers, plain turquoise and pink would go well with it; or cream and red with a background of brown looks most effective.

Try to use materials of the same weight; cotton is the best material for patchwork. It is firm to sew and washes well.

Finally, try cushion covers first before attempting a quilt!

Some points to remember

When Making Bed Quilts

(1) Wadding is usually 18 ins wide. For a 6 ft long bed, 3 ft wide, you will need 4 yds of washable wadding or 8 yds if you want to make the quilt thicker.

(2) You will need between 6 and 10 reels of sewing thread for stitching the quilted design for a single bed quilt.

(3) Top covers can be cotton, linen, denim, silk, satin, gingham, seersucker or fine wool. It is preferable to use washable wadding for quilting—it is light and easy to use.

General Hints

(1) Spend a lot of time tacking the three layers of material into place and dividing the material into 3-in or 4-in squares.

(2) If you are using the pattern lines to quilt along, work from the front of the material. If you are sewing squares, triangles or any other design unrelated to the top material, mark this design with tailor's chalk on the backing material and work from the back.

(3) When quilting patchwork, oversew all the patches together until the work is the correct shape. Tack the wadding and backing material into place and sew along the seams through all three materials. Finally embroider along the seams or trim with ric-rac braid.

(4) When making an appliqué design, draw the shapes directly onto the material. If the design is to be repeated several times, draw it first onto paper, then transfer it to the material with dressmaker's carbon paper.

It is possible to sew dramatic and effective accessories for our homes and for ourselves by machine quilting. Although it is sometimes said that this form of quilting lacks some of the originality of the traditional quilter's work, this need not necessarily be so. By considering and making best use of the modern materials available, bed quilts and other items can be machine-made and still have the quality of individualism which is the basic principle of an heirloom—and after all quilting has its roots in practicality. Sometimes the addition of simple motifs of appliqué or embroidery will help to create a craftsman-like object thus combining the use of a machine for sewing the bulk of the item with the hand-sewn finishing touches.

Formerly sheep's wool was washed and carded and placed between the two outer layers and this method is still used by a few Welsh traditional quilters. Sometimes old, thin blankets were substituted and this made an attractive new bedcover without incurring too much expense. Nowadays cotton wool or kapok can be used but washable wadding is easier.

Many examples given in this book

cannot be copied exactly since the material you will use will be different. The directions for making up the basic item are given and the photographs will indicate the sort of suitable materials to choose and the way to set about quilting your own material in order to achieve an exciting result.

All the machine quilting in this book was done with an ordinary electric sewing machine without the use of any accessories.

Denim Quilt

This quilt is intended for a teenager's room which perhaps has to double as a study, so the material needs to be of a modern design and to be hard-wearing and practical.

Materials
4½ yds denim 48 ins wide
4 yds washable wadding
2 yds flannelette 36 ins wide
6 reels sewing thread

Instructions Cut a length of denim 3 ins longer and 3 ins wider than bed, i.e. for a 3 ft bed 6 ft long, cut a piece 39 × 75 ins.
Cut wadding to exact size, say 3 × 6 ft. Since this is usually 18 ins wide, open the wadding up and use two layers. Place the denim right side down, pin

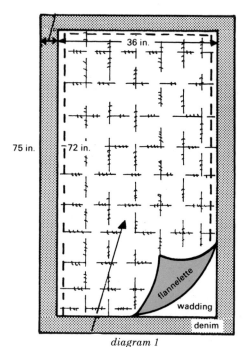

diagram 1

diagram 2

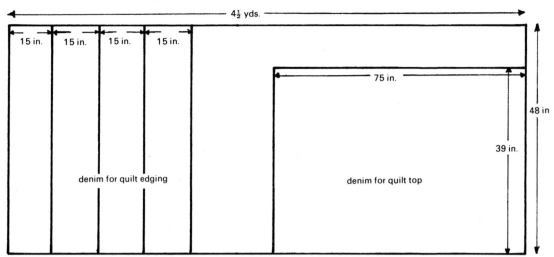

diagram 3

the wadding and flannelette in place leaving a 1½-in margin on all sides. Tack around the edges, then horizontally and vertically in 4-in squares, so the material will not ruck up. When quilting something of this size, time is well spent tacking the material prior to stitching, since the three layers will be quite heavy. (See diagram 1.)

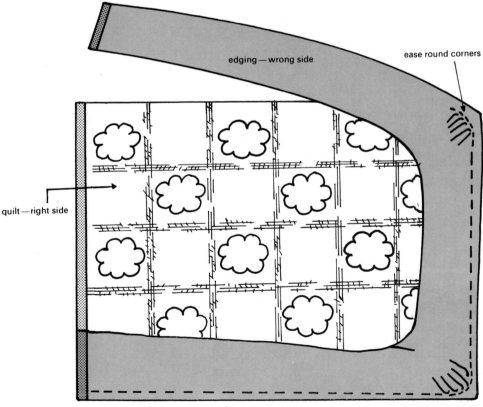

diagram 4

In the example, the circles were stitched round, then some of the dots were joined up, across and down the material. In places these formed four squares, which emphasized the check motif within the circle. (See diagram 2.) Cut the remainder of the material into strips 15 ins deep, across the material. (See diagram 3.) Join these into a long strip of material 15 ft long. Hem the top 1½ ins of the quilt over the wadding and flannelette. With right sides facing, tack the edging to the quilt on three sides, easing in the material round the bottom two corners. Machine stitch these sides into place leaving a 1½-in seam (i.e. sewing along the sides of the

wadding and flannelette which have been measured to fit the exact edge of the divan). (See diagram 4.)
Hem the inside edge over the wadding and flannelette as you did for the top to give a neat finish. (See diagram 5.)

Note
The sides of the quilt could be narrower or deeper, depending on the height of the divan. If the room is also used as a study, buy another yard of the material and make a quilted day case for the pillow. Make this case up according to the instructions for the red-striped cushion cover on page 101, to your pillow size.

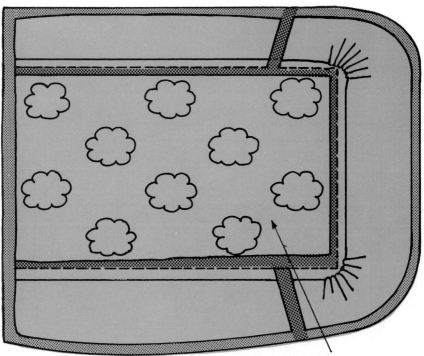

back of quilt (flannelette)

diagram 5

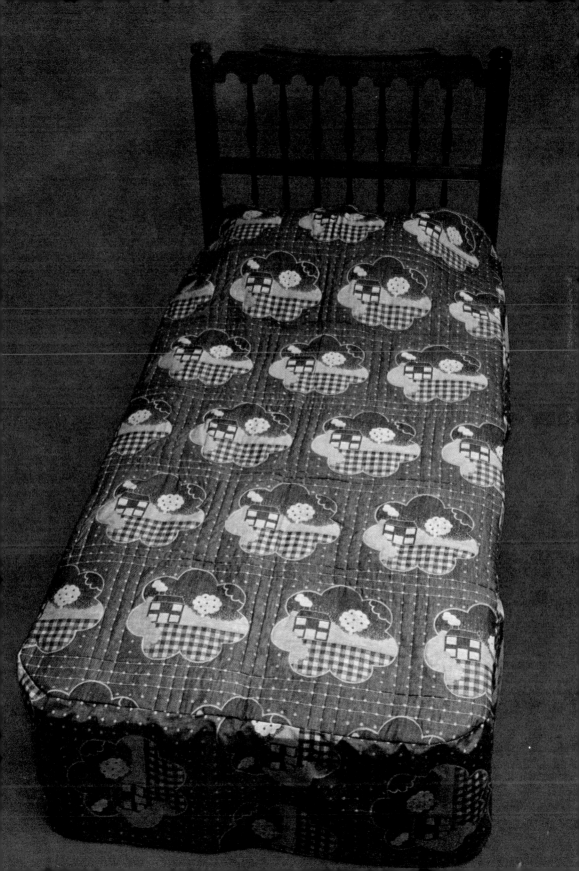

Simple Marriage Quilt

Materials

4 yds gingham
4 yds cambric backing material
1 yd white cotton
10 reels white sewing thread
Lace, braid etc. for trimming motifs
15 yds ric-rac braid
8 yds washable wadding, for 32 squares,
  cut for double thickness

Instructions

Cut 16 squares 16 × 16 ins in gingham.
Cut 16 squares 16 × 16 ins in cambric.
Cut 32 squares 15 × 15 ins in washable
wadding for double thickness.
With right sides facing, machine sew
one gingham square to one cambric
square on three sides ($\frac{1}{2}$ inch seam
allowed), making a pocket. (See
diagram 1.) Turn right side out.

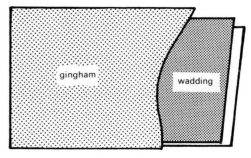

diagram 2

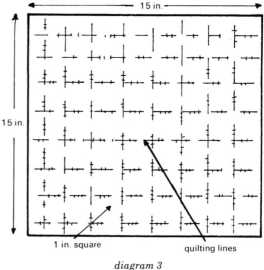

1 in. square   quilting lines

diagram 3

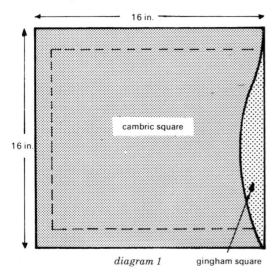

diagram 1   gingham square

Slide two layers of wadding carefully
into pocket. (See diagram 2.) Fold in
the $\frac{1}{2}$ inch hem along the top and neatly
oversew. Repeat this for all 16 squares.

Then machine stitch each square in
1 inch squares to form the quilting.
(See diagram 3.) Cut eight squares
12 × 12 ins in the white cotton and
eight squares of wadding 11 × 11 ins.
Place a piece of wadding at the back
of the cotton and tack a hem $\frac{1}{2}$ inch
round. (See diagram 4.)
On these medallions, appliqué gingham
symbols, relating to the couple for
whom the quilt is being made. The
appliqué designs can be enhanced by
the use of lace, braid or embroidery.

80

Then appliqué these eight medallions onto eight of the large gingham squares. (See diagram 5.) Use any variety of stitches in the appliqué work. Oversew these panels together alternately with one plain gingham square. As the quilt is quite heavy, it is best to oversew from the front of the quilt, then again at the back to ensure the seams are strong.

Heart: a traditional motif on a quilt of this type.
Candle and matches: a useful item to include in remote areas! These open at the tops and I have enclosed a small candle and book matches.
Sporran: to indicate money and the hope that they will always have some. This, too; opens at the top and I have enclosed a small coin in it.

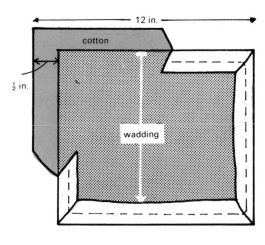

diagram 4

diagram 5

Machine sew the ric-rac braid on the seams and lastly around the outside of the quilt to make a neat finish. (See diagram 6.)

Notes
This example was made for a young couple who live in a remote village in Scotland, so the motifs appliquéd to the quilt were as follows:
Circle: to symbolize a wedding ring, with the couple's names embroidered inside, together with the date of their marriage.

Pottery: for the husband is a craftsman potter.
Boat and Book: for the wife is a travelling art teacher–visiting remote schools, some only accessible by boat.
Fish: since their new home is on the edge of the sea and fish will be part of their harvest.
Apple: because they hope to become self-sufficient, growing all their own fruit and vegetables.
This will give you some idea and no doubt you will have great fun thinking up your own symbols.

diagram 6

Red Quilt

This luxurious looking quilt was made simply by choosing quite an intricately patterned material but quilting it in squares.

Materials
For a 3ft. divan bed, 6ft long
$4\frac{1}{2}$ yds material 36 ins wide
4 yds washable wadding
2 yds muslin or flannelette (for extra warmth)
6 reels sewing thread

Instruction
Cut a piece of material 75 ins long.

Cut the wadding and backing material to exact size – 36 × 72 ins. The wadding is usually 18 ins wide, so open it up and use two layers.

Quilt Top
Place the material right side down, pin the wadding and backing material in place. Tack round the edges. With a straight edge and tailor's chalk, mark the backing material with the lines to be stitched by measuring the material into 3 in squares. (See diagram 1.) Tack along these lines making sure the material does not ruck up either at the front or back. Using a contrasting

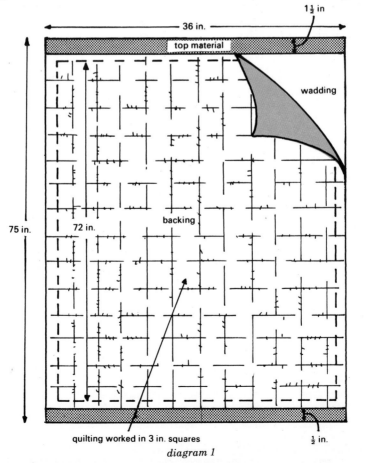

36 in.

$1\frac{1}{2}$ in

top material

wadding

75 in.   72 in.

backing

quilting worked in 3 in. squares

$\frac{1}{2}$ in.

diagram 1

colour cotton (gold was used on this red material), machine stitch along all these lines. Hem 1½ ins over top edge, covering the wadding and backing material.

Sides of Quilt

Make a length of material 18 ins deep and 15 ft long by neatly stitching five 18 × 36 ins panels together.

To make the crenellated edge, with the wrong side facing, mark out as follows.

Every 6½ ins draw a line 3 ins deep from the edge. Cut up the 3-in line and make mitred corners. (See diagram 2.) Stitch a hem along the bottom and around the crenellations. (See diagram 3.) With right sides facing, tack and stitch the edge along the side of the quilt (i.e. tacking along the sides of the wadding and backing material, which will fit the exact edge of the divan). ·

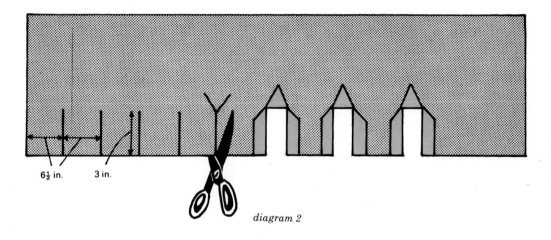

6½ in. 3 in.

diagram 2

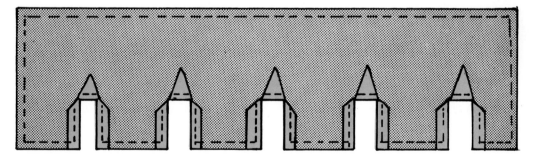

diagram 3

overleaf, Red quilt

Girl's Appliqué Quilt

Materials
1⅔ yds nylon
1⅔ yds backing
1⅔ yds washable wadding
Sewing thread
½ yd gingham
Remnants of cotton material for figure
Stranded embroidery thread in green,
    orange or brown (or colours to match
    your own choice of material)

Instructions
Cut all three materials to
32 × 57 ins. Place wadding between
nylon and backing. Tack round edges,
taking care the material does not ruck.
Quilt in diagonal lines. Cut 2 in wide
lengths of gingham and join to make a
16 ft length. With right sides facing
machine stitch around edge of quilted
material. Turn over and hem on back
of quilt.

Girl Figure
Cut out the shapes. (See patterns
overleaf.)
Use similar materials for the bonnet
and pinafore, gingham for the dress,
sleeve and petticoat and black net
for the boots.

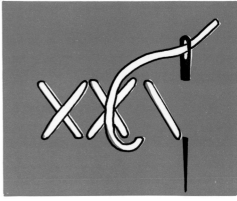
Cross Stitch

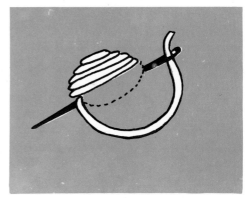
Satin Stitch

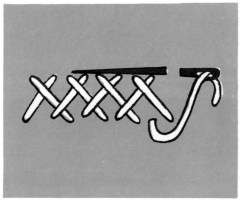
Herringbone Stitch

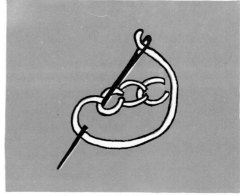
Chain Stitch

Red Quilt

Using the templates, cut one of each shape, allowing a $\frac{1}{4}$ inch turning. Tack hem, carefully remove templates. Pin the pieces into position on the centre of the quilt. Hand stitch around the edges. With contrasting embroidery thread, embroider round the edges, using stitches shown here.

Embroidery is not usual in quilting but is commonly used in appliqué work to emphasize the design and make a more exciting motif. Embroider the flowers in place.

Notes

This effective appliqué could also be applied to ready quilted material if desired. A deep box edging could be added as in the denim quilt. This could be of a matching material to curtains in the bedroom, and could also be used in the girl's dress, if the design was small enough.

⟨⟨⟨⟨⟨⟨⟨ Herringbone stitch

XXXXXX Cross stitch

∞∞∞∞∞∞∞ Chain stitch

Satin stitch

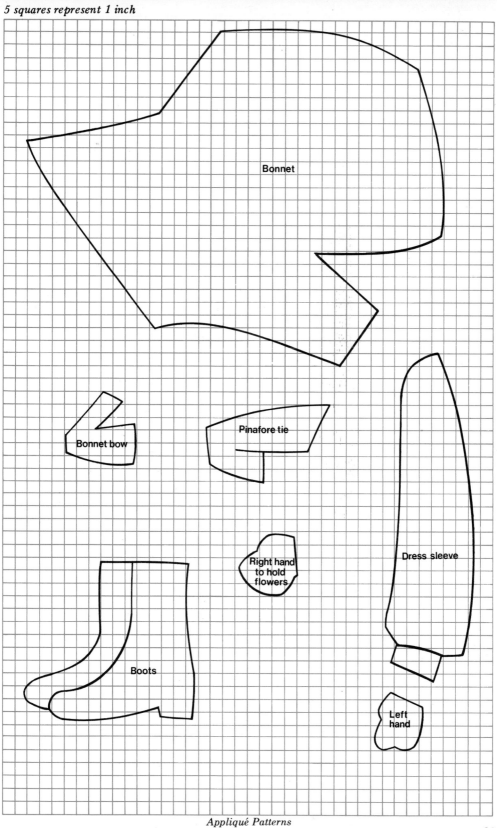

Bonnet

Bonnet bow

Pinafore tie

Right hand
to hold
flowers

Dress sleeve

Boots

Left
hand

Appliqué Patterns

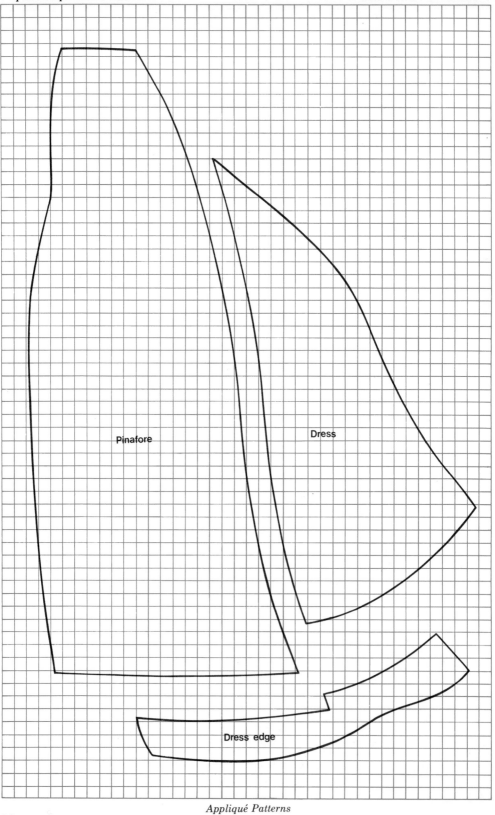

Pinafore

Dress

Dress edge

Appliqué Patterns

Patchwork Quilt

Materials

2-in square templates

Scraps of cotton material, enough for 648 squares

35 yds ric-rac braid

5 yds cotton lawn or seersucker made into a strip 10 yds × 18 ins

2 yds 36-in wide cotton material for backing

2 yds 36-in wide washable wadding

Sewing thread

Embroidery thread

Instructions Cut out 50 2-inch square templates from thin card. More can be made later. Assemble the scraps of materials you intend to use. Cotton is preferable.

Remember to follow a colour scheme right through the quilt. Here purples, greens and blues were chosen. Cut squares of material about ½ inch bigger all round than templates to allow for turning.

Tack material to templates (see diagram 1.)

Lay tacked patches on a table and arrange them to best advantage, putting a plain one next to a patterned one throughout the work. With

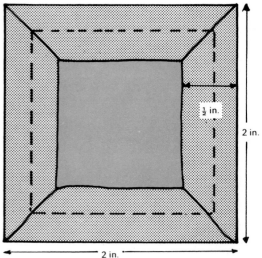

diagram 1

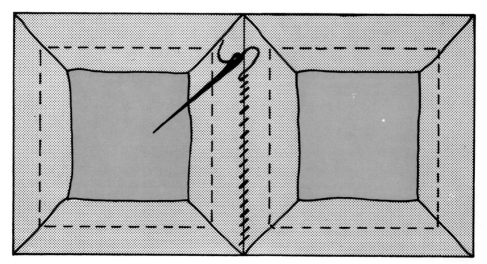

diagram 2

ordinary sewing thread oversew
patches together on wrong side with
small stitches (see diagram 2.)
The quilt can be built up as you
acquire more material of suitable
colours. To make the quilt for a single

together and then machine along the
lines of the patchwork, Feather stitch
down seams on right side (see diagrams
3 and 4).
Stitch the ric-rac braid into position,
through all three layers, dividing the

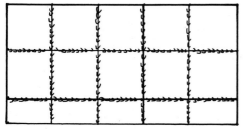

feather stitch between squares

diagram 3

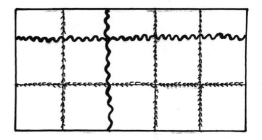

diagram 5

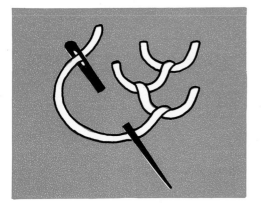

diagram 4

diagram 6

bed, it will need to be 18 patches across
by about 36 down the length. When all
the patches are sewn together place
the patchwork right side down on the
table. Place the layer of washable
wadding on top and then the backing
material. Tack the three layers

patchwork into sections of 9 patches
(see diagram 5).
Make frill of cotton lawn or seersucker
18 ins wide to go around three sides of
the quilt, leaving 3 ft edge for the top of
the bed. Machine in place.
(See diagram 6.)

overleaf, Patchwork quilt

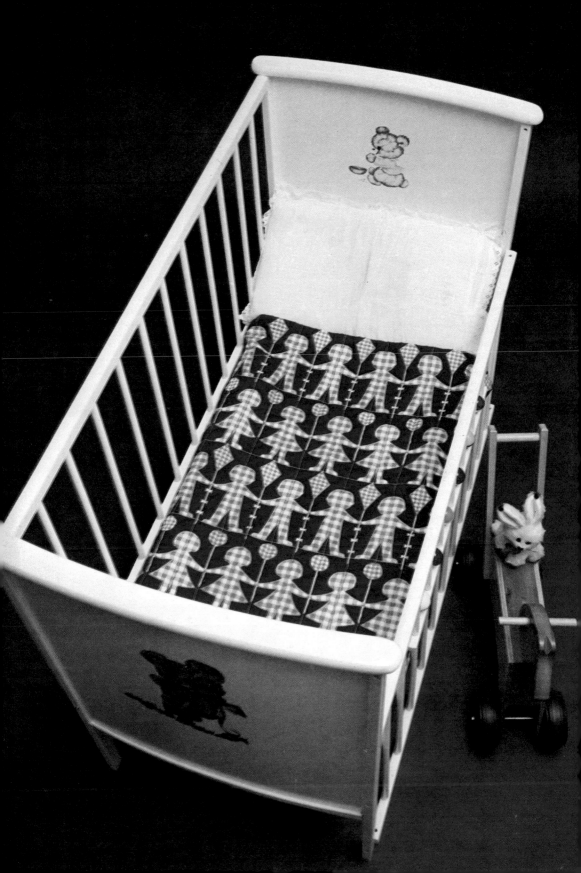

Cot Quilt

In choosing suitable material for a cot quilt, look closely at the wide selection of children's furnishing fabrics. The material used in this example was printed with gingham figures which appeared to have been appliquéd when the material was quilted.

Materials

1 yd material 48 ins wide

Washable wadding 30 × 42 ins

1 yd 48 ins wide or 1¼ yds 36 ins wide backing material cut to size 30 × 42 ins (cotton, terylene cotton, muslin, etc.)

8 reel sewing thread

tack in position. Place the backing material exactly on top of the wadding and tack in position, sewing carefully through the three layers. Tack several lines down and across the material so that it does not ruck up when machining. (See diagram 1.)

With the correct side facing, stitch round the shapes you have decided to use to build up the quilted effect on your material. In the example shown, squares were sewn, following the lines of the kite strings down the material and the feet of the figures across. Finally stitching was done around the figures achieving the double effect of

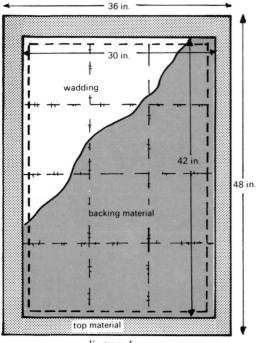

diagram 1

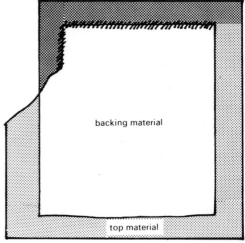

diagram 3

quilting and appliqué work. (See diagram 2.)

When quilting is finished stitch the cotton ends through and secure at the back.

Hem the 3-in excess top material over the washable wadding and backing material to make a neat finish. (See diagram 3.)

Instructions Place material right side down on table, place the wadding on top leaving a 3-in margin on all sides,

preceding page, Cot quilt

diagram 2

Notes

This same idea could be carried out for older children, using suitable fabric and making the quilt larger. Materials printed with planes, cars, trains etc. could be quilted in squares and oblongs. Animals could be treated in the same way as the figures if they formed a bold design, or they could be surrounded by circles and ovals.

If the quilt is to be used in a pram, a matching pillow-case could be quilted. Alternatively, some of the material could be used to pipe the edge of a white pillow-case and one figure could be appliquéd to the top corner.

Large Square Cushion

Materials

2½ ins hexagon template

Odd scraps of material left over from dressmaking, etc

2 yds 36 in strong cotton material for lining, and underside of cushion

6 skeins stranded embroidery thread to tone with one colour in the patchwork

It is sometimes advisable to buy some small amounts (about ½ yd of each) of plain cotton material to make a balanced patchwork pattern, picking out colours in the printed pieces you intend to use.

Instructions

Using the 2½ inch hexagon template (see diagram 1), cut out 40 templates in thin card. Cut pieces of material about 1 inch bigger than template all round to allow for turning. Carefully tack material to templates making sure that the material is smooth and tight. This is very important with large patches as the work will pucker when sewn together.

Assemble the covered templates on the table, and move them around until you have found a design you like; you will find the possibilities endless. It is

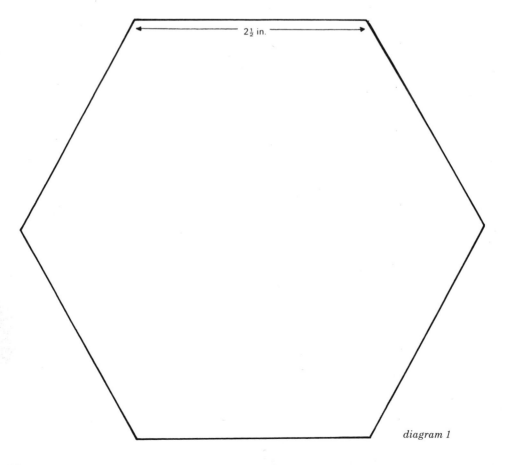

2½ in.

diagram 1

essential to decide on a pattern before you start to join the work together. Oversew patches together with sewing thread using small stitches for extra strength. It is easier to start with the centre patch and work towards the edges. (See diagram 2.) To make the

the piece of patchwork. Lay lining on table then patchwork exactly on top, right side up, and place the piece of backing material on top. Tack the three layers firmly together on three sides, and then machine. (See diagram 4.) Turn right side out. Place the cushion

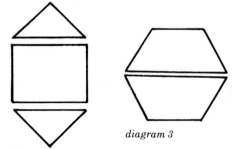

diagram 2

cover square, cut several templates in halves and triangles (see diagram 3), cover and sew into place at the edges. When all the patches are sewn together take out tacking and templates, and press well.
Then with three strands of embroidery thread, feather stitch (see page 93)

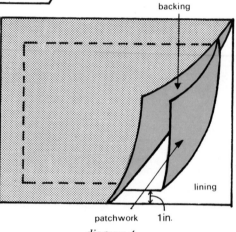

diagram 4

between the backing material and patchwork lining. Oversew the fourth side.
If you want to quilt the cushion then you should follow the quilting instructions earlier in the book. Stitch the wadding into place between the patchwork and the lining and do the quilting before you tack the backing into place.

diagram 3

all seams where patches have been stitched together.
Now cut two pieces of plain cotton material 1 inch larger all round than

Quilted Cushions

Look for interesting materials with definite lines to sew along – curves, diagonals, checks, stripes etc. and build up the pattern from there. This is a good way to use beautiful remnants which are always just too small to make a skirt or a blouse.

RED OBLONG CUSHION

Materials

1 yd striped material 36 ins wide, cut into two equal pieces 36 × 18 ins

Washable wadding 34 × 16 ins
Muslin 34 × 16 ins

Instructions In this example the stripe in the material was made good use of in the quilting. The wadding was tacked on the back of one piece of the top material (though you could, of course, buy double the amount of wadding and backing and quilt both sides of the cushion), then the muslin backing was tacked in place, leaving

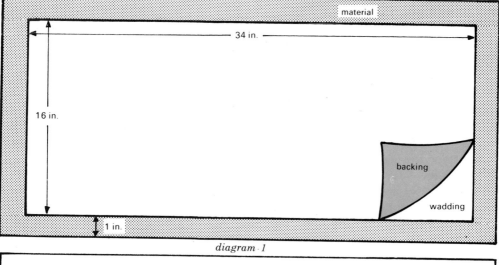

diagram 1

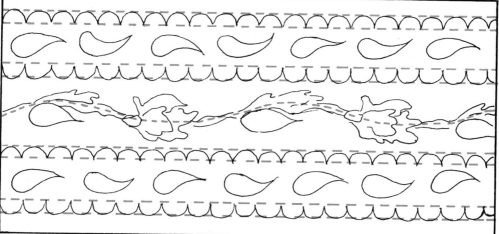

diagram 2

diagram 3   hem these edges

a 1 inch margin on all sides. (See diagram 1.) With the top side facing, sewing was done down the vertical lines of stripes, then following the line of the stalk of the flowers in the wider panel. (See diagram 2.)

To Make Up a Quilted Cushion
Take the quilted piece of material and hem the 1 inch excess material over the wadding and the muslin at the top (narrow) edge only. With the other piece of material hem one narrow edge only. Take both these pieces of material and with right sides facing, machine stitch 1 inch away from edge on the remaining three sides (i.e. on the edge of the wadding). (See diagram 3.) Hem this edge over the wadding and muslin (as the top edge). Turn right side out. Insert cushion filling and sew along open end.

FLOWER CUSHION

This was made from a remnant of curtaining fabric, printed with two bold flower-like designs side by side. The wadding and muslin were stitched in place as for the red cushion, but the material was not cut into two and both

diagram 4

flowers were quilted in an identical manner. (See diagram 4.) With right sides facing, the seam was made by machining carefully around the edge of the wadding, leaving a small petal unsewn. The cushion was put inside, then the small petal carefully oversewn. This cushion has a patchwork quality when quilted because of the different coloured layers of petals.

Quilted flower cushion
see p. 106 for red oblong cushion

102

Round Cushion

Materials ·

2 ins hexagon template

Scraps from dressmaking, etc., both plain and printed

$1\frac{1}{2}$ yds plain cotton material for lining, and underside of cushion

6 skeins stranded embroidery thread (used here: 1 pink, 2 purple and 3 green)

2 or 3 press studs

Instructions

Cut 19 2-inch templates in thin card. Now cut 19 pieces of material 1 inch larger than the templates;

1 plain purple for centre patch;

6 printed pieces for joining to centre patch;

12 pieces in green to join to printed pieces;

12 pieces in purple triangular shape cut from template for the edge of the work. (See diagram 3 page 100.)

Tack material carefully to templates, and arrange pattern on the table ready for sewing.

Starting in the centre, oversew six printed patches around plain centre purple patch. Now sew twelve green patches to printed ones. Next sew on purple triangle templates to form a round shape. (See diagram 1.)

From printed material, cut a long piece 3 ins wide and $1\frac{1}{2}$ yds long. Gather to fit round edge of cushion, tack and machine on.

Take 3 strands of stranded embroidery thread in pink and feather stitch on join between printed patches.

With 3 strands of purple, feather stitch

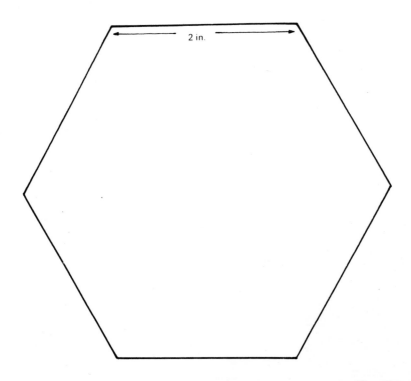

2 in.

all round purple centre hexagon, and round triangles on the edge of the cushion.

Lastly, with green stranded thread, stitch round the three sides of the green patches.

Cut out piece of plain cotton material 1 inch larger round than the finished patchwork. This piece is for the lining. To make a split back in the cover, cut circles wrong side up exactly on the patchwork and lining, so that one edge overlaps the other in the centre. Tack the three layers together carefully and then machine.

Turn the cover the right way out, and press the seam at the edge. (See diagram 3.)

Stitch two or three press-studs along back seam opening.

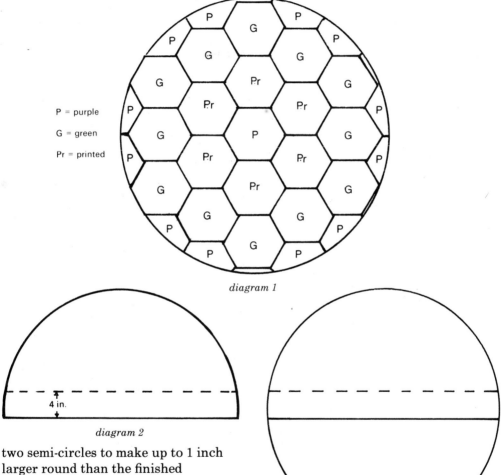

diagram 1

P = purple

G = green

Pr = printed

diagram 2

4 in.

diagram 3

two semi-circles to make up to 1 inch larger round than the finished patchwork, but allow 4 ins extra on the straight side to allow for flap-over. (See diagram 2.)

Machine 2-in seams on straight sides of semi-circles.

To assemble cushion, place lining on table and then patchwork right side up exactly on top. Now put the two semi-

If you want to quilt the cushion, do so in the same way as you would for the square patchwork cushion.

Oven Gloves

Materials
$\frac{1}{2}$ yd cotton and $\frac{1}{2}$ yd towelling both
 36 ins wide
Pieces of white tape
White sewing thread

Instructions Cut out pieces of each material 27 × 18 ins. With wrong sides facing, quilt this material in diamonds, squares, stripes or whatever is suggested by the fabric. (See diagram 1.) Fold the quilted material in half and cut a rectangular shape 26 ins long and 7 ins wide. (See diagram 2.) From one piece cut a square in the centre (see dotted lines on diagram 2), resulting in two glove backs and one

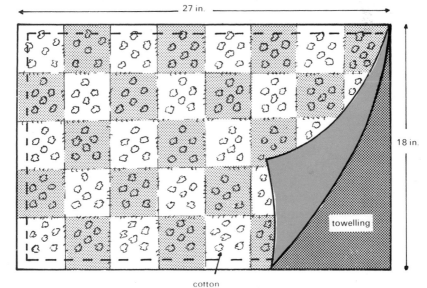

cotton

diagram 1

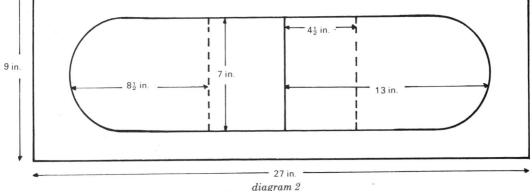

diagram 2

Round cushion and quilted red oblong cushion

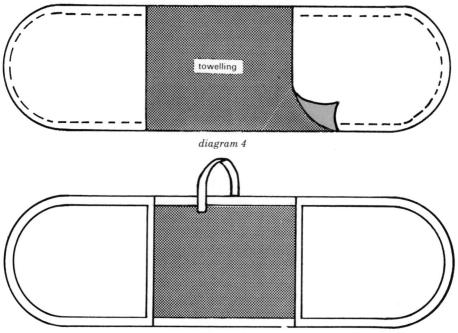

diagram 4

diagram 5

square pot holder. Hem both the glove backs at the straight edge (wrist). Use the pattern piece shown in diagram 3 to shape the ends of strip and glove backs. With the wrong sides (towelling) together tack both the glove backs in place on the other long piece. (See diagram 4.)

With the remainder of the unquilted cotton material make a long strip of material 1 inch wide. With the right sides of the strip and oven glove front facing, machine right round the edge. Turn over and hem on the towelling side. Add a loop of tape in the centre so that the gloves can be hung near the cooker. (See diagram 5.) The square piece cut from the middle of the glove

back should be edged in the same way and a loop added to make a pot holder.

Pot Holder

overleaf, Oven gloves

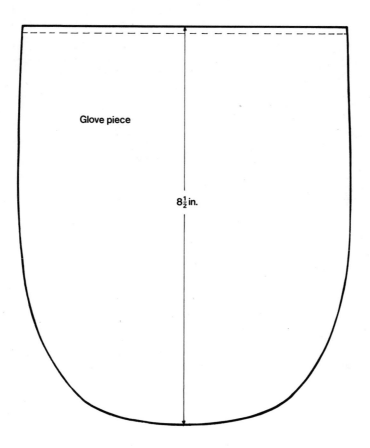

Glove piece

$8\frac{1}{2}$ in.

diagram 3

Pyjama Case

Materials
½ yd nylon material
¾ yd washable wadding
½ yd backing material
1 Swiss cotton handkerchief
White sewing thread
2 yds nylon ribbon

Instructions Cut two circles each of
nylon, and backing, and three circles of
wadding about 14 ins across or about
1½ ins larger all round than the
handkerchief.

diagram 2

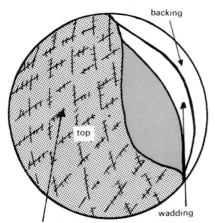

diagonal quilting lines

diagram 1

Make one side of the case by laying one
circle of the wadding between one circle
each of nylon and backing. Stitch the
three circles together in diagonal lines.
(See diagram 1.)
Repeat for the other side of the case.
Pin a circle of wadding to the back of
the handkerchief. Tack into position.
Machine stitch round the design
printed on the material (see diagram 2).
Trim the wadding back to the exact

edge of the handkerchief. Finally pin
the quilted handkerchief on to the
right side of one of the sides of the case
so there is a 1½ inch margin on all sides.
Machine stitch around the edge of the
handkerchief. (See diagram 3.) With
the wrong sides facing machine stitch
about two-thirds of the way round the
bottom part of the sides, leaving
¼ inch margin. (See diagram 4.) Trim off
excess material carefully. Turn inside

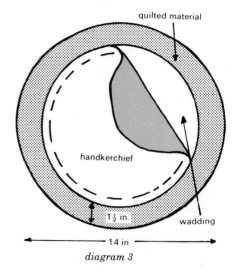

quilted material

handkerchief

1½ in.

wadding

14 in

diagram 3

preceding page, Pyjama case

112

out and restitch this seam, making a French seam. Hand stitch the nylon ribbon to the right side of the pyjama case. (See diagram 5.) Turn and hem it on the inside. In this example lemon nylon ribbon was used, since the quilted case was white on the outside and lemon on the inside.

Notes
You could also use ready-quilted material as a base if you wanted to save time. The material could be patterned, in which case the centre design could be of a single contrasting colour material with a random stitch quilted design on it.

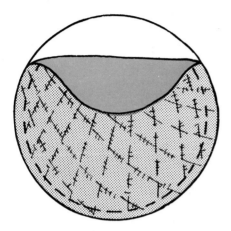

diagram 4

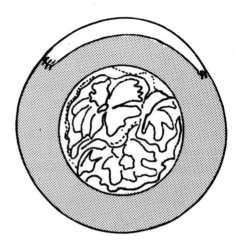

diagram 5

Beach Bag

Materials
1½ yds 36-in cotton material
1½ yds 36-in towelling
1 yd white cord
2 × 14 in open ended zips

Instructions Cut the cotton material
to 54 × 28 ins.
Cut the towelling to 52 × 22 ins.

Place the two sides together (wrong
sides facing) with the towelling placed
in the middle of the cotton. Hem this
surplus cotton back onto the towelling
to give a wide attractive border.
(See diagram 1.)
Machine sew the pattern onto the
towelling to give a quilted effect.
(See diagram 2.)

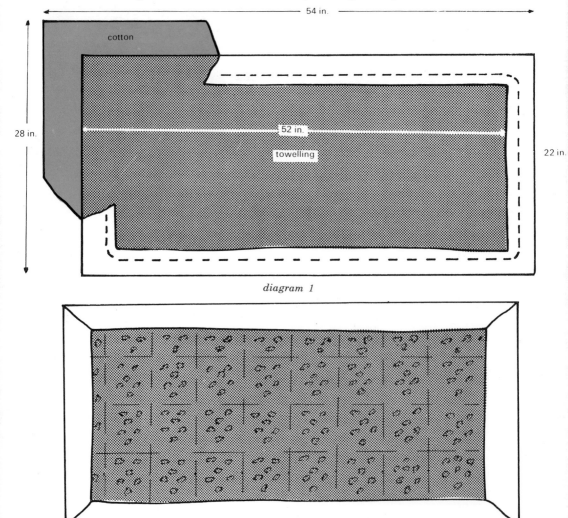

diagram 1

diagram 2

Place the material down, towelling uppermost, fold in the sides to a depth of 10 ins. (See diagram 3.)

Sew the open ended zips in from
A–B and B–A
C–D and D–C
Sew handles into place, making sure to sew through only one layer of the material. Tuck the ends into the bag.

Notes

This is a very useful beach bag, large enough to take all the family's swimming things (see diagram 4) but unzip it and you have a useful beach 'blanket'.

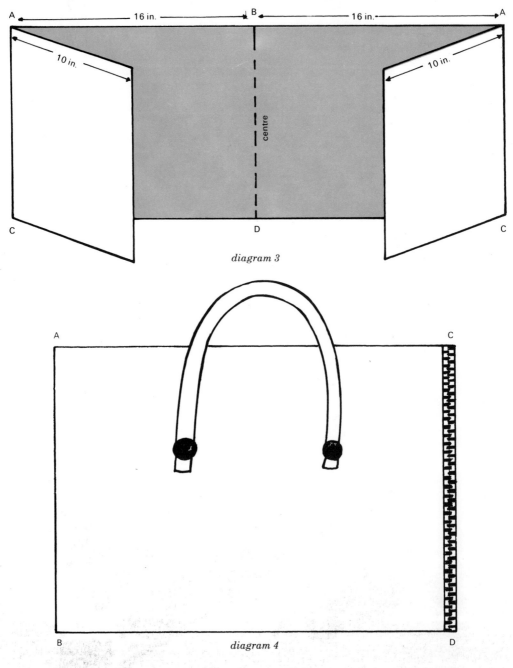

diagram 3

diagram 4

Batik Picture

This modern wall-hanging was made from a batik print. A more traditional one could be made from a tapestry print. Batik is a very easy and attractive method of printing and well worth trying.

Materials
Piece of pure cotton material
2 paintbrushes
Old saucepan containing melted batik wax, household candles, beeswax or combination of all
Cold water dyes
A tjanting (not essential)

crack it a little, so that the dye will penetrate the waxed areas slightly. Dye with a cold water dye, following the maker's instructions. When the dye has taken, wash out the surplus dye and dry the material. Iron between layers of brown paper to remove the wax, thoroughly wash in detergent and dry. This process can be repeated to get third and fourth colours but, when choosing a colour scheme, remember the colours in batik must get progressively darker! You can't dye dark blue–yellow!

In this example, start with a square of

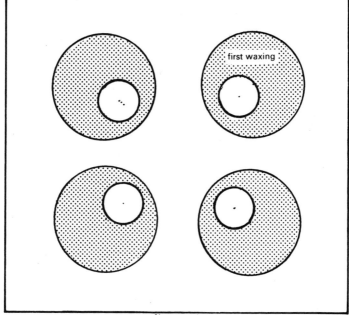

diagram 1

Instructions Draw a pattern in pencil on the square of pure cotton. Paint the areas to remain the original colour of the material with hot wax, making sure it is hot enough to soak through to the back of the fabric, using a paintbrush or a tjanting. When the wax is cold,

yellow cotton. Draw the circles, paint them with wax and dye the material green (with a blue dye). (See diagram 1.) Remove the wax, clean the material and repeat the process, covering the areas you wish to remain yellow and green with wax, but instead of using a

117

paintbrush use a tjanting to get an abstract effect. Use a brown dye. (See diagram 2.)

To Quilt

Pin a piece of wadding to the back of the finished print and tack it into place.

Begin by sewing round the circles, then the squares and finally some of the random tjanting strokes. (See diagram 3.) Finally, secure to a simple frame. This, of course, is only a small batik. If you had the time to do a much larger one, you could make a brilliantly artistic bed quilt.

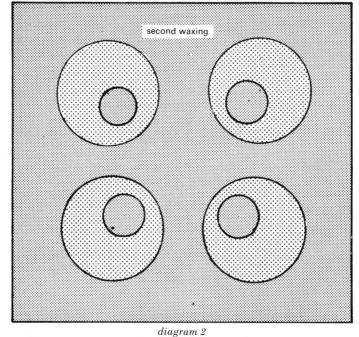

diagram 2

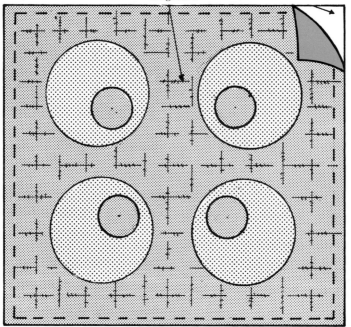

diagram 3

Bib

Materials
¾ yd cotton print
½ yd towelling
Elastic
½ yd washable wadding

Instructions Cut two sleeves. (See diagram 1.)
Cut one front pattern in each of three fabrics (cotton, wadding and towelling). (See diagram 2.) Take the three fronts and tack together in the right order, i.e. with the wadding in the middle. With front side facing, quilt front panel (See diagram 3.)

diagram 3

Sleeves: Join sleeve seams and hem wrists, leaving ½ inch unstitched so that elastic can be threaded through. Tack front of sleeves to front panel.

Sew together.
With bias binding or piece of top material cut on the bias, stitch round neck, back of sleeve, round edge of bib, back of second sleeve to neck again. Turn and hem on the back. Add two tie tapes at the back neck and insert elastic in cuffs. Diagram 4 shows bib made up.

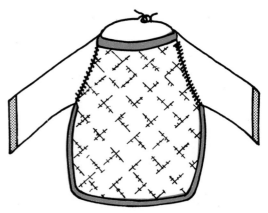

diagram 4

Notes
For a young baby this could be made of towelling at the front and a fine plastic at the back. This example was made in a cotton print with a backing of towelling. For older children it could be made in a practical fabric, backed with plastic for use when painting or playing messy games. This pattern could easily be adapted for larger and smaller sizes.

overleaf, Bib

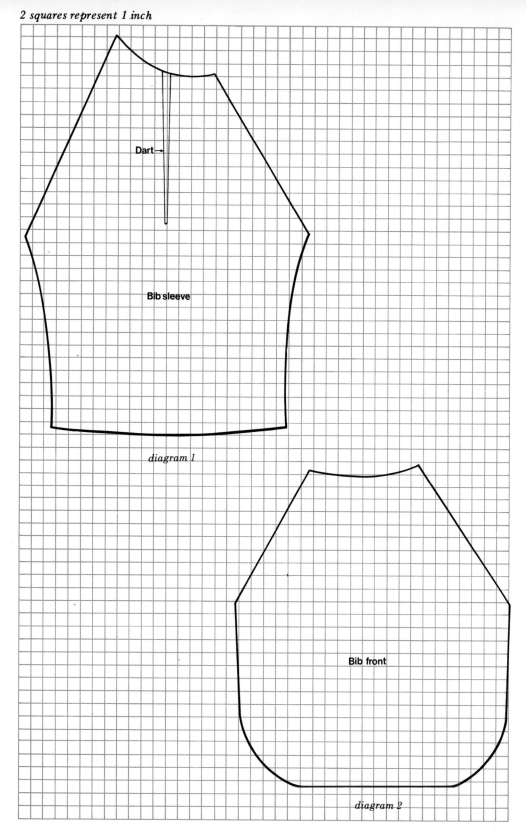

Dart→

Bib sleeve

diagram 1

Bib front

diagram 2

Reversible Jacket

This example was made in corduroy and jersey but there are endless combinations. You could also use fine wool, suede, leather or tweed for everyday wear, velvet and brocade for evenings or cotton and towelling for use on the beach.

Materials

Use a simple jacket pattern to make the waistcoat and buy the amount of material stated in two different fabrics. In addition you will need two buttons and half a yard of washable wadding.

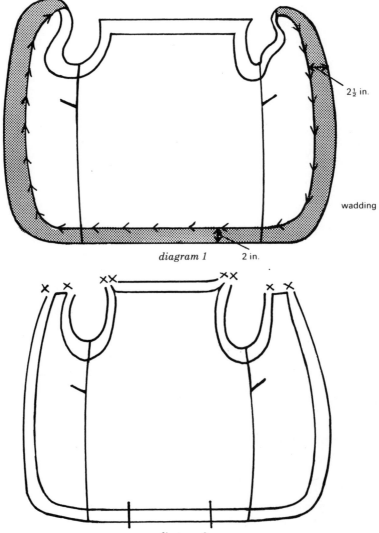

diagram 1

diagram 2

preceding page, Reversible jacket

Instructions Cut out two fronts and a back in each of the materials. Machine stitch bust darts of all four fronts. With right sides facing, join the two fronts to the corresponding back in each material. Press seams.

Cut out two sets of the wadding shape for quilting. This is a strip which follows the outside outline of the jacket to an inner depth of $2\frac{1}{2}$ ins on the fronts and 2 ins on the back. Pin the wadding round the edges of the fronts and along the lower edges of the back on the wrong side of the material. Tack and machine along the inside lines (see arrows indicated on diagram 1). Mark the pattern to be quilted in diagonal lines and then quilt along these.

Join the two waistcoats together by placing them right sides together and stitching as follows: (see diagram 2).

(1) Back of neck leaving $\frac{1}{2}$ inch unstitched at shoulder.
(2) Around armholes leaving $\frac{1}{2}$ inch unstitched at shoulder.
(3) Top fronts leaving $\frac{1}{2}$ inch unstitched at shoulder.
(4) Bottom fronts and along lower edge leaving 6–8 ins unstitched in the middle.

Clip all curves.

Carefully pull the garment through the gap in the lower edge so it is the correct way. Press very carefully. Machine stitch shoulder seams together

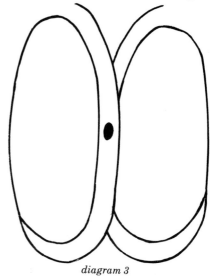

diagram 3

on one fabric with right sides facing. Hand sew shoulder seams together on other side by turning in the seam allowance and slip stitching the edges together. Slip stitch the lower edge gap together neatly.

Make the button-hole and stitch a button on either side of the jacket so that it does up on either side. (See diagram 3.)

Pinafore Dress

Materials:
Use a simple pinafore dress pattern, making sure it has a yoke. You should buy the amount of material stated. You will also need some washable wadding.

Instructions Cut the yoke pattern out twice. With right sides facing, sew the seams on the shoulders and around the neck. Turn the right way and press. Cut a piece of washable wadding slightly smaller than the yoke pattern and slide it gently into place. Tack around the neck and armhole edges. Machine sew the pattern on the yoke. On this dress the lines of the yoke were followed in order to emphasize them. (See diagrams 1 and 2.)

Since the material was a very fine lawn, a narrow edge of washable wadding was stitched horizontally along the bottom tier.

A similar design to diagram 2 was also sewn across these lines regularly around the hem (See diagram 3.) The dress was then put together according to the pattern. If a dress with a quilted yoke is to be sleeveless, then the armhole edges can be neatly turned towards the centre and stitched together, or bound with a piece of matching material cut on the cross.

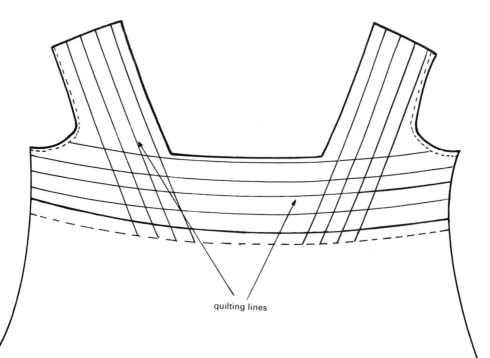

quilting lines

diagram 1

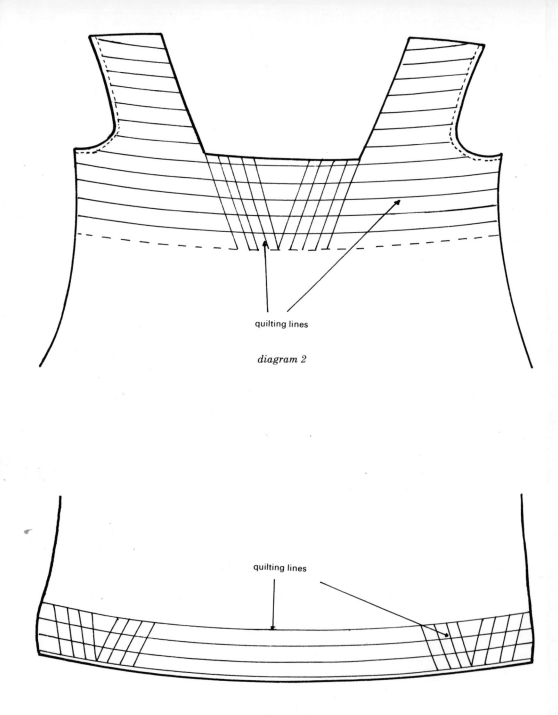

quilting lines

diagram 2

quilting lines

diagram 3